C

A Diversity of Dante

A Diversity of Dante

by Thomas Goddard Bergin

RUTGERS UNIVERSITY PRESS

NEW BRUNSWICK, NEW JERSEY

Permission to reprint has been kindly granted by the following publishers:

Appleton-Century-Crofts—all English translations of the Comedy not otherwise credited. They are from *Dante Alighieri: The Divine Comedy*, Translated and Edited by Thomas G. Bergin. Copyright © 1955, Appleton-Century-Crofts, Division of Meredith.

The Cesare Barbieri Center of Italian Studies—"The Women of the *Comedy*," by Thomas G. Bergin, from *Cesare Barbieri Courier*, Vol. VII, No. 2, Spring 1965.

Indiana University Press—"Hell: Topography and Demography," by Thomas G. Bergin, from *Essays on Dante*, ed. by Mark Musa, Bloomington, 1965.

The Mediaeval Academy of America—"Dante's Provençal Gallery," by Thomas G. Bergin, from *Speculum*, Vol. XL, No. 1, January 1965.

The Virginia Quarterly Review—"Dante's *Comedy*—Letter and Spirit," by Thomas G. Bergin, from Vol. VII, No. 2, Autumn 1965.

The Yale Review—the sonnet "Dante," by Thomas G. Bergin, reprinted from *The Yale Review*, copyright Yale University, Vol. LV, No. 1, Autumn 1965.

To Thomas Caldecott Chubb
for many reasons

Acknowledgements

The sonnet "Dante" originally appeared in the *Yale Review*, Vol. LV, No. 1, Autumn 1965.

"Dante's *Comedy*—Letter and Spirit" first appeared in the *Virginia Quarterly Review*, Vol. VII, No. 2, Autumn 1965.

"Dante's Provençal Gallery" is here reprinted, with some slight modifications, from *Speculum*, Vol. XL, No. 1, January 1965.

"Hell: Topography and Demography" is included in *Essays on Dante*, edited by Mark Musa and published by the Indiana University Press in 1965.

"The Women of the *Comedy*" was first published in the *Cesare Barbieri Courier*, Vol. VII, No. 2, Spring 1965.

I am grateful to the editors of the *Cesare Barbieri Courier*, *Speculum*, and the *Virginia Quarterly Review* as well as to the Indiana University Press for permission to include these items.

"Citizen Dante" is, in substance, a lecture given originally to the undergraduates of the State University of New York at Albany in 1960. "Light from Mars," slightly revised, was prepared as a lecture given at Catholic University of America in 1965. "*Paradiso* IX" is the hitherto unpublished English text of an essay which, translated into Italian and edited by my friend the late Professor Siro Chimenz, was printed as a *fascicolo* of the *Nuova Lectura Dantis*, Rome, A. Signorelli, 1959.

All translations in this book, from whatever source, are my own, unless otherwise noted. A number of the passages from the *Divine Comedy* are from the edition of Appleton-Century-Crofts, New York, 1959, here reprinted by permission.

Contents

Acknowledgements   *vi*

"Dante"—a sonnet   *x*

1. Concerning a Greek Princess, a Florentine Jokester, and the Uses of Diversity—Introductory   *1*

2. Dante's *Comedy*—Letter and Spirit   7

3. Citizen Dante   *24*

4. Hell: Topography and Demography   *47*

5. The Women of the *Comedy*   *65*

6. Dante's Provençal Gallery   *87*

7. *Paradiso* IX   *112*

8. Light from Mars   *143*

Notes   *167*

Index   *173*

A Diversity of Dante

Dante

He saw his townsmen haloed in the light
Of vast eternity; he saw God's ways
In frail flesh manifest. Through bitter days
Of banishment he kept his vision bright,
Grew lean with labor through the lonely night
To distill prophecy from ancient lays
And fuse the flowing verse with golden phrase.
He probed old wrongs to point to us the right
And long lost pathway through the savage wood.
Whence came his warrant? Was it all because
The Twins lent him their glory from the skies?
From rancor at injustice grew this good—
Truth's champion proscribed by evil laws—
Or was it born in Beatrice's eyes?

—*Thomas Goddard Bergin*

1

Concerning a Greek Princess,
A Florentine Jokester, and the Uses
Of Diversity—Introductory

ತಾ

In one of the less prepossessing zones of lower Hell and, it must be confessed, in one of the less attractive cantos of the *Comedy*, two minor figures make their hasty entrance before the eyes of the poet. The somewhat ponderous simile which introduces them serves to sharpen the effect of their precipitate intrusion on the scene as well as to prepare us for their acts of irrational violence. Its complicated rhetorical structure too stands in contrast to the complacent and somewhat malicious confidences of the garrulous alchemist, with which the preceding canto has terminated. But let the poet now speak for himself.

> When Juno was enraged 'gainst Theban blood
> Because of Semele, as more than once
> She showed, then Athamas became so crazed
> That as he saw his wife, on either arm
> Bearing a son, approach, he roared: "Spread wide
> The net so I may catch the lioness
> With both cubs at the pass," and, stretching out
> His arms, with talons pitiless he seized
> The one child named Learchus, whirled him 'round
> And dashed him 'gainst a rock, whereat his spouse
> The other with herself drowned in the sea.

And when harsh Fortune cast the Trojans down
With all their pride that once had been so bold,
Then Hecuba, sad, captive and forlorn,
Fresh from the sight of slain Polyxena,
When she espied her Polydorus dead
Upon the shore, for very madness bayed
Like any dog, so sorrow wrung her soul.
But Furies, whether Trojan or of Thebes,
Never committed an act so inhumane,
Even in goading brutes much less men's limbs,
As I beheld performed by two pale shades
All naked who ran biting right and left
As a hog does when let out from his sty.
One reached Capocchio and in his neck
Fixed fangs so deeply that it dragged him on
Scraping his belly on the hard earth floor.
The Aretine all trembling left alone
Explained to me: "That rabid little gnome
Is Gianni Schicchi, who in maddened rage
Goes goring other souls." And I to him:
"So may his partner's teeth leave you untouched
Say who it is before it skip away."
The answer came: "Yon is the ancient shade
Of vicious Myrrha, who beyond the bounds
Of rightful love felt passion for her sire.
With sinful purpose she would visit him,
Taking another's likeness, as did he
Who now departs, intending so to win
The lady of the troop. He falsified
Buoso Donati, drawing up his will
And validating his last testament."

                                        (*Inferno* xxx, 1–42)

A pair of falsifiers, then, and of the worst kind, for they are
not falsifiers of gold, as are counterfeiters and alchemists but
of their very persons, pretending, for their own illicit ends, to
be other individuals. They fall into place well enough and we
accept them as exemplifying Dante's love for categories and

putting the right things (or souls) into the right place. We also are prepared to accept, without overmuch demur, the superficially odd grouping of a classical and a contemporary figure. After all, this is Dante's normal procedure, an evidence of his drive for syncretism, an aspect of his persistent purpose to make us see mankind as one, whatever may be the contingencies of time and tradition that might seemingly divide it. Have we not remarked that Francesca comes forth from the company of which Dido is one, that Obizzo d'Este and Alexander are bathed in the same river of blood, that Curio and Mosca are in the same *bolgia* and similarly mutilated? Still, there is perhaps more to be said about the pair in Canto xxx. Not only do they come from a different tradition; they are also of different sexes, and, very strikingly I think, their personalities and their stories belong to very different levels of sentiment and esthetics; recounted in detail their histories would have an impact not so much of contrast as of irreconcilable dissidence. For the legend of Myrrha, the doomed princess, is a somber tale of perverse passion, suggestive of tragedy and perhaps of primitivism, while Gianni Schicchi's little game can arouse only laughter and is an apt subject for treatment for Boccaccio. Myrrha bespeaks anguish and despair, Gianni Schicchi is a confidence man; the ill-starred girl emerges from the dark mythological mists of pre-history, the plausible trickster can be found in the anecdote columns of any metropolitan newspaper.

One could find no better example in the *Comedy* of Dante's almost obsessive search for diversity of *exempla* to establish the integrity of an ethical principle, or, in another sector, to make of the most disparate elements a firm and consistent artifact. The *Comedy* is a cunningly contrived weaving of various colors and designs, resulting in one irridescent and consistent texture. With the fusion of the classical and the Judaeo-Christian traditions we are all familiar, and we have accepted too as a part of his scheme the intrusion of the contemporary; these things are matters of substance. But the tones too are noteworthy for their harmonizing of seemingly discordant themes: somewhat similar to Gianni Schicchi and Myrrha is the pair cited as examples of good zeal in *Purgatorio* XVIII, where in two startling lines the visitation of Mary is linked with the military exploits of Caesar. But such examples are all but trivial when we think of the bold mixtures of modes and moods recurrent throughout the poem: the pastoral imagery which introduces the terrible procession of living torches in *Inferno* XXVI, the austere Cato bidding the poet to go wash his face, the preoccupation (shocking in a saint if we but stop to think of it) of old Cacciaguida with the Florence of his youth. Linguistically, too, evidences of this same calculated daring are not hard to find. Who else would dare to put baby talk into a grave homily on time and eternity (many translators shy at translating the *pappo e dindi*—nursery words for "bread and money"—of *Purgatorio* XI because in English it would sound too silly), or have the venerable Solomon speak of the joy the blessed souls will have in seeing their "mammas" —not "mothers" but "mammas"—on Judgment Day. Who else would have permitted a sinner to say (it is the best equivalent): "This to you, God!"? Politically Dante may have preferred a stratified, hierarchical society, but there is an underlying democracy in his esthetics. There is room for all, not only Christians, pagans, and Moors; not only the prominent personages, through whom, faithful to Cacciaguida's instructions, he drives home his ethical lessons, but also the incidental yet no less memorable peasant who leads his flock to pasture in early spring, the tailor peering through his needle, the hillbilly gawking at his first sight of the city.

And surely the gamut of humors and tempers is as complete as the range of *personae*. The noble wrath of a Folquet de Marseille, the sad resignation of a Brunetto, the sweet serenity of a Piccarda—these are evocative of sober meditation—but there is room too for the mischief of the *Malebranche*, the sly unvoiced chuckle of the hypocrites, the complacency of a Sapia, even the engaging indifference of a Belacqua. Dante's vision of humanity is total. Is it purely poetic, even solely philosophical—or is it not also an aspect of the didactic drive which characterizes all of his works? In the *Convivio* he tells us he wants an audience—and furthermore not an audience of intellectuals only; he writes the *De vulgari* because he feels instruction on such matters is necessary and useful; the *De monarchia* springs from a burning desire to convey a political thesis. I believe our poet not only wanted an audience but that he wanted the widest possible audience; he is writing not for clerics only (else he would have used Latin) but for all who care to read—or it may be even for those who, being illiterate, can merely listen. It has been well said that one reason at least for the choice of *terza rima* was that it was at once easy to memorize and hard to mutilate or garble. I believe that, as Dante wanted, so far as was possible, to put all kinds of men and moods into his poem, so also he wanted to be heard by all kinds, ranging from "donna Berta e ser Martino" up to "German Albert" himself, whom he addresses directly in the personal invective of *Purgatorio* VI.

Believing this, I am not inclined to apologize for the nature of this *Diversity*, however imperfect its component parts may be. I do not think it an unworthy thing for an interpreter of Dante—or, let me speak more openly and without shame, a lover of Dante—to spread abroad the message of the poet and, if possible, inculcate admiration for him, in whatever way or at whatever level may seem appropriate. Four of the items this book contains were originally given as lectures, three of the four to audiences for the most part made up of undergraduates, receptive, alert, and well read but by no means "Dante scholars." The others, though in varying degree, are somewhat more specialized. I hope the latter group will not be entirely tedious to the neophytes in the study of the *Comedy*; I dare even hope that the former group will be adjudged not entirely worthless by *dantisti* (a brotherhood, I may say, in the main made up of tolerant spirits, for the love of the poet binds us all together). I like to think that the presentation of such an *antipasto* is not foreign to the spirit of the *Comedy*; if, as an *antipasto* should, it whets the appetite for the main course and sends the reader scurrying to the *Comedy* itself, this will indeed fulfill my highest wish. And surely the figure needs no apology: the poet himself wrote: *Messo t'ho innanzi; omai per te ti ciba* (I've set the plate before you; feed yourself).

2
Dante's *Comedy*—Letter and Spirit

Dante's great poem has enchanted and one might say hypno-
tized scholars for centuries, and library shelves groan with
books, pamphlets, and monographs on every aspect of the
work, from "Light Metaphysics in the Paradise" down—or
from a human point of view possibly up—to "Ambiguities of
the Three Beasts in the Wood." The nature of Dante's art in-
vites such studies, which often provide valuable insights.
But however erudite such investigations may be, the real
challenge to the critic, it seems to me, lies in the area of
synthesis. For the poem is everything: a personal confession, a
vast love lyric, an encyclopedia of the knowledge of the Middle Ages, a precious historical document, a zealous exposition
of dogma, and of course quite simply an absorbing narrative.
It is also ornamented with all the seductive rhetorical devices
which a poet can possibly use to embellish his work. Or,
should we choose to focus on the man behind the word, consider for a moment the contrasts and contradictions of the
poet himself. He is the most approachable of major poets, as
T. S. Eliot has remarked: his grammar is simple, his appeal
immediate. He is also the most subtle. He is the most learned
of poets, making use as he does of every literary and cultural
tradition that has preceded him; and at the same time he wrote
his great work not in Latin, not even in the high style of the

vernacular, but in the frank, everyday speech of the people, colloquial and even at times coarse. He is by nature partisan and passionate, but at the same time he has such a sense of discipline that he never loses sight of his plan. He is the most universal of poets, for his subject deals with man's action on earth and his eventual destiny in the hereafter, with Good and Evil, with Life and Death, with Time and Eternity. But he is also the most parochial; Florentine political intrigue of the late thirteenth and early fourteenth centuries absorbs him, and the affairs of his neighbors, petty and transient, are built into his transcendent vision of the cosmos. It is this last paradox which presents the greatest problem to the critic and reader of the twentieth century. How far must we go in exploring Dante's world if we are to understand him? To what extent must we be medievalists or Thomists? Giovanni Papini laid it down that no one could understand Dante who was not a Florentine and a Catholic, but I think the persistence of the poet's fame among those not so privileged as Papini has given the lie to that. On the other hand Carducci, happily also a Tuscan, has stated baldly, albeit in verse, that Dante's twin pillars of the medieval Church and Empire leave him completely indifferent yet the poem still holds him in rapt admiration. This too was the attitude of Lowell and, I believe, the vast majority of Dante's readers; we may, then, here note in merely summary fashion the facts of his life and times that may help us to place the poem in its context.

Our poet was born in Florence in 1265 under the sign of the twins (some time between mid-May and mid-June). He died in Ravenna in 1321. During his whole lifetime there was no political stability in Italy. The papacy had triumphed over the Empire and had in turn come under the thumb of the rising power of France and in 1309 was carried off to Avignon for some seventy years of captivity. The Italian cities, meanwhile, in the power vacuum thus created in the peninsula, were conniving and clawing their way to independence and prosperity. Dante disapproved of all these things: he wanted the Empire restored, he wanted the papacy purified and the King of France humbled. He wanted his own city more disciplined. A Guelph—that is, a papalist—by inheritance and a Ghibelline— an imperialist—by conviction, he was unable to survive in the turbulent political life of Florence, in which he played, though briefly, a leading rôle, and in 1302 went into exile.

As for literary influences, Dante was both a scholar and a poet. He was well versed in Latin, knew the *Aeneid* by heart, and was familiar with all the classical works current in his day. He also had extensive knowledge of the poets of the lyric tradition—the Provençal and his own countrymen. He knew the epic poems in old French and the didactic works of his predecessors, typified by Brunetto Latini.

He had read the mystics and the commentaries of St. Thomas Aquinas (who died a decade after Dante's birth); the rational Aristotelian exposition of dogma for which St. Thomas was noted had a great appeal for our poet. And here we may add the footnote that in Dante's time faith was by no means monolithic. If it was the age of Thomas it was also the age of the Albigensian and Catharistic heresies, the age of the evangelical Franciscans, who may be regarded in some ways as premature Protestants, and the age of widespread atheism among certain elements of the aristocracy.

Now Dante being—again a paradox—very much of his time while yet truly a man for the ages, he reflects all these currents, political and intellectual. If he had never written the *Divine Comedy* he would be still a major figure in Italian literature. But it is the *Commedia* that is his true monument and must claim our attention here. Let us take up the very simple and fundamental questions: what is the *Comedy*, what is the author's purpose in writing it, and what are its treasures for us? Or to phrase the last question again: quite simply why is it a great poem, as meaningful and as beautiful in the twentieth century as it was when circulated in manuscript among the intellectuals of our poet's own day?

As to the nature and purpose of the poem we may well

begin with Dante's own words. In his celebrated letter to Can
Grande della Scala he writes as follows: "The subject of the
whole work, taken according to the letter alone, is simply a
consideration of the state of souls after death; for from and
around this the action of the whole work turneth. But if the
work is considered according to its allegorical meaning, *the
subject is man, liable to the reward or punishment of Justice,
according as through the freedom of the will he is deserving
or undeserving.*"

And from Dante's own lips again we may add two corolla-
ries: one from the *Convivio* to the effect that a composition
must have beauty as well as a message if the reader is to be
attracted, another from the *Vita nuova* that the literal meaning is never to be despised or distorted but must be able, as it
were, to stand on its own feet.

The best approach to the poem, I think, is to follow Dante's
own prescription and work through the literal. Probably even
those who have not actually read the *Comedy* are familiar
with the outline of the narrative: the hero lost in a wood, his
rescue by Virgil, and their descent together into the world of
the damned; their progress from horror to greater horror,
through whirlwind, flame, and ice, until at the very center of
the earth they confront the source of evil, Satan himself; then
their subsequent climb through the terraces of Purgatory, the
encounter with Beatrice at the summit, her "taking over" of
our purified pilgrim, and the ascent through the spheres of the
blest to the ultimate vision through which Dante himself is
carried on for a precious time—or is it eternity?—with "the
love that moves the sun and all the stars.

It is sufficient to recount the "beautiful fiction" in capsule
form to indicate the attraction of the story *qua* story. It has all
the appeal of science fiction in its presentation of worlds unknown to us and exciting to our imagination. It has continuous
motion, the pace never lags. Dante has the secret too of fusing
pattern and variation. All of the realms are concentric circles,

all with appropriate subdivisions; after a while you are aware of an overriding design but within it what ingenious variety! Now the wayfarer is met by a group of sinners, now by merely one. In one terrace of Purgatory no one sees Dante, in another the penitents are immediately aware of the presence of a living man. There are dramatic cantos, narrative cantos, lyric cantos, cantos of exposition. Masterly too is the device of a companion and a guide. Dante always is *with* someone, Virgil or Beatrice or St. Bernard, who can instruct him, reason with him, discuss with him, and, on occasions, participate with him. And our hero himself, intent through Hell and Purgatory on keeping the promised rendezvous with his love, eager there and elsewhere for information to pass on to you and me, constant in those respects and in his all-embracing curiosity, is infinitely varied in his reactions; now frightened, now confident, now thoughtful, now cheerful, often reflective but occasionally amused, scornful of some souls, compassionate of others, and, alas, downright cruel to yet others. And finally what a wealth of realistic touches to convince you that the literal is indeed factual! Telling of how old Cavalcanti emerged from his tomb, to cite but one example, he says: "I think he had raised himself upon a knee." Surely, the reader's subconscious tells him, this man had been there. If he were only making up a story he would have said "Cavalcanti got up on his knees." But naturally his memory is not too good, he cannot be quite sure. The precision of this remembered detail makes it clear at once that Dante had in fact *been there*.

Nor is this all. Beyond everything else, I think, on the literal level, the reader is won by the abundant humanity of Dante, his perception, his compassion, his deep understanding of the human heart. This is artistically exemplified in the gallery of unforgettable characters, as rich as and perhaps more varied than those of Shakespeare. Let one example here suffice to illustrate the depth of subtlety of his characterization, which also opens the way to allegory and doctrine. For many years the most famous episode in the *Comedy* has been the story of Francesca, and I do not think we would be wasting our time if we dwelt on it for a while.

When Dante meets Francesca he is still relatively a newcomer in Hell. He has been through the vestibule, he has crossed the Acheron in a swoon of terror, and he has fraternized with the virtuous pagans in Limbo. But now he is to confront sinners fixed in their sin for all eternity. He learns that, borne on the eternal tornado which deafens his ears, without hope of rest, are the souls of the "carnal sinners who subjected reason to desire." With the journalistic impulse that characterizes his attitude throughout the entire trip, he notes down the names as Virgil calls the illustrious roll: Semiramis, Dido, Cleopatra, Helen of Troy, Achilles, Tristram, Paris. But a pair unnamed by Virgil catches his eye and, encouraged by his mentor, he asks them "in the name of their love" to come and speak to him. Mercifully and very exceptionally the infernal hurricane eases off and allows Francesca to speak. Grateful for Dante's compassion, she tells her tragic tale, how

> "Love which lays sudden hold on gentle hearts
> Seized him for my fair body, torn from me
> In such a fashion as to grieve me yet.
> Love, which absolves no heart beloved from loving
> Seized me so strongly for the joy of him,
> That I am still its captive as you see.
> Love led us both together to one death."
> "Caina waits for him who quenched our lives."
>
> (*Inf.* v, 100–107)

But this does not quite satisfy our probing reporter. He wants to know the circumstance, the occasion of Francesca's tragedy. And Francesca replies, in perhaps the most celebrated passage of the *Comedy*:

> There is no greater pain
> Than memory of happy times gone by
> In wretchedness—and this your teacher knows.

> But if you have such eagerness to learn
> The first roots of our love, I'll do as one
> Who tells a story, weeping as he speaks.
> One day, it chanced, for pleasure, we were reading
> Of Launcelot and how love bound him fast;
> We were alone, of all suspicion free.
> That reading more than once compelled our eyes
> To meet and caused our faces to change color,
> But it was one point only that undid us:
> When we read how one deeply cherished smile
> Was kissed by such a lover—it was then
> That this soul, who shall never leave my side,
> All trembling kissed me full upon the lips . . .
> A Gallehaut was the book and he who wrote it
> And in it we no further read that day.
>
> *(Ibid.,* 121–138)

Let us here, before we are carried away by the humanity of
the tale, make a few purely literary comments. We know
from certain names on Virgil's list that we are in the realm of
courtly love; the passion, and one might say the religion, of
love, typified in the Middle Ages by the story of Launcelot
and Guinevere, of Tristram and Isolde, is our subject here.
With his usual honesty, Dante acknowledges his sources when
he has Francesca tell us that it was in fact the story of Launcelot that she and Paolo were reading. He does more than that.
In Francesca's original statement, "Love which lays sudden
hold on gentle hearts," he reaffirms the basic credo of the
school: that only the noblest hearts are worthy of love (an
incidental tribute to his predecessor Guinizelli—*Al cor gentil
ripara sempre amore*—Love ever seeks the gentle heart);
when again she says "Love, which absolves no heart beloved
from loving," he expresses an axiom of that school that true
love, granted a noble heart on each side, was bound to be re-
ciprocated; when she says "Love led us both together to one
death" Dante is perhaps indirectly voicing the judgment of
the moralist on this kind of passion; equally likely he is reveal-

ing the death wish that the modern critic Denis de Rougemont has found to lie in the heart of the medieval love cult. And, from a purely stylistic point of view, the repetition of "love" is poetically effective and psychologically the key to Francesca's soul.

All of these things could have been put into the mouth of Guinevere or Isolde, the standard "types" of the medieval love-tradition. But Dante takes a case from contemporary society. And this, I think, so that we may understand that such tragic affairs are not merely something read in books; they are very real, they can happen to people of our own world; it is easy to see Isolde as a heroine, but what if it be a lady we know? Little is known actually of the story of Francesca; one account says that she was married, without having met him, to Gianciotto, an unpleasant and deformed warrior, the handsome younger brother Paolo serving as proxy. Every attenuating circumstance was hers; doctrinally she illustrates the marginal case: she is no venal Cleopatra, no wanton Semiramis. But, for all that, she has sinned and, alas, been cut down with no time for repentance. So Dante the writer and judge puts her here as a particularly piteous example of those "who have subjected reason to desire." But is that the whole story? No, since Dante the wayfarer swoons with pity. And then we remember that the poem is only literally a picture of souls after death; the true revelation is of those now living. And here is a love-tossed soul, buffeted, feverish, at war with itself, hardly happy, yet choosing above all things fidelity to love and the loved one. Francesca is gentle, noble, and, in spite of what society will call her, faithful. Yet she is guilty too. In Hell she must be if the laws of society are to prevail, but the law of love is not always that of society.

Other magnificent figures of Hell there are who have the same rich ambiguity. Farinata, the proud aristocrat, the fanatical political partisan, comes to mind. Dante the writer and judge puts him among the damned, but Dante the pilgrim and the human being gives him stature and grandeur. Or take the case of Pier della Vigna, the trusted chancellor of the great Emperor, who, in despair at having lost the favor of his master, committed suicide. Again, for a suicide there is no salvation and damned Pier must be through all eternity. But with what sympathy Dante hears his tale of court intrigue and jealousy and the context of envious malice that had brought about his downfall! Taken collectively, such portraits—and there are others—dramatize the concept of sin as it is presented in Hell, and, being of real people and not merely stock "types," bring out Dante's allegory of souls in this life. The lustful, the ambitious, the despairing, they have indeed lost "the good of the intellect" and pay heavily for it. Yet how magnificent some of these obsessions are! Though Dante never forgets his dogma, yet again and again in the *Inferno* he allows—quite consciously, I think—his humanity to transcend it.

The gallery of portraits is richer in the *Inferno* than in the other two parts of the poem. Some critics have drawn from this the melancholy conclusion that only sinners are really interesting people; the great bulk of creative literature would tend to support this—from Adam and Eve on down. But in fairness to our poet it must be added at once that there are fascinating and complicated characters also in the *Purgatorio*, full of penitents who yet retain some trace of the earthly, and even in the *Paradiso*, where some of Dante's saints show a lively and theologically unbecoming interest in political affairs and contemporary gossip. But I think that what happens as we move from the night of Inferno to the dawn of Purgatory is that imperceptibly Dante himself takes over as the main character. In Hell all was new, strange, and of course frightening. Further, our hero was continually under the dominance of Virgil, who had been there before, who knew the road, and was seldom surprised by anything encountered on the way. In the *Purgatorio* Virgil is no longer supreme. This is a realm he has never entered before and although of course Dante is also a stranger here, yet the fact that he is a Christian gives him an advantage over Virgil. So perforce his personality comes more to the fore. Furthermore, both literally and on the allegorical level, while Dante in the *Inferno* could contemplate, condemn, or condone, he could not participate. Dogmatically the damned are cut off from us forever; on the narrative level the sinners in Hell are souls whom, whether they be admirable, contemptible, or indifferent, Dante will never see again; in the terms of his allegory they portray deviations which he has no desire to imitate. But in the *Purgatorio* he is among his own kind; within the framework of the tale these are souls who are going his way and with whom he will spend eternity; allegorically they are the living souls whose intentions are firmly fixed on their own spiritual healing; they are the illuminated ones who, no matter how feeble their endowment, how weak and frail they may be, are using their will (and free will is the key to salvation) to refine and purify themselves. With these souls Dante temperamentally, philosophically, and existentially can associate; doctrinally he not only *can* but *must*. So we find him bowing his head as he plods along with those burdened with pride, blinded as are the other penitents by the dark cloud of wrath, fearfully entering the purging flame in the cornice of the lustful. The natural conditions of Purgatory too are appropriate to a living man; here is no subterranean hollow in the earth where sun, moon, and stars shed no radiance—for that matter here is no world of outer space like Paradise, where the earth looks like a grain of sand in the distance. Here, rather, is alternating benevolent sunshine and refreshing darkness. Perhaps, as certain sharply etched pictures of humanity are typical "Hell poetry," certain descriptions of nature are characteristic "Purgatory poetry." Here is twilight, not so much seen as sensed in a mood, a passage incidentally which inspired Gray to write his elegy:

> It was the hour which homeward turns the thought
> Of those who sail the sea, and melts their hearts
> If that day they have bade dear friends farewell,
> Piercing with love the novice pilgrim's breast

When from afar he hears the chime of bells
That seem to sorrow for the dying day.
                                    (*Purg.* VIII, 1–6)

Nature, our own earth, which we her children must love, is
refined and exhibited in all her beauty in the passage of Canto
XXVIII descriptive of the earthly Paradise. Dante has just been
informed by Virgil that he has nothing more to learn from his
beloved teacher and his own free will is now his best guide.
This is an allegory, of course, of the restoration of innocence
after penance and, given an historical twist, it puts Dante in
the position of Adam. And the passage is an evocation of the
garden of Eden (which Dante, never willing to leave the
pagans out entirely, equates with the legend of the golden
age). All this and more subtle symbolism may be read into it,
as well as the purely psychological allegory of sweet repose
after achievement. But the initial impact is simply one of
beauty, which can be felt, I think, even in translation:

Already moved to enter and explore
The God-made wood, green and luxuriant,
Which tempered the new daylight to my eyes,
I left the hillside without more delay,
And crossed the mead with lingering steps and slow,
Treading upon the aromatic earth.
A gentle breeze that in itself contained
No variation blew against my brow
With no more force than tender zephyr bears.
The branches, quick to quiver in response,
Were bending all in unison towards where
The first shade of the Holy Mountain falls,
Yet they were not so far from being straight
That all the little birds up in their tops
Gave up the practice of their varied art;
Nay, but in singing with full gladsomeness
They welcomed the first breezes 'midst the leaves,
Whose murmuring made the burden to their rhymes.
                                    (*Ibid.*, XXVIII, 1–18)

In this background then, a little more lovely but still very much like the world we live in, in this new freedom to participate and to face Virgil as a friendly peer, Dante's personality expands and takes the center of the stage. And so yet another allegory, his personal one, is apparent to us, and by the time we reach the last cantos with the coming of Beatrice we are prepared for Dante's confession and we know that all that has gone before had a special and personal application as well as a general one. It was, we knew, Everyman's story and so ours; now we are made aware that it is Dante's too.

The *Purgatorio* with its freedom and its humanity is an appropriate place to discuss various aspects of life as we live it in our own world, which is also one of effort and hope. In the *Inferno* most of Dante's questions were factual: who are those spirits? what river is this? what is Fortune? *et cetera*. In the *Paradiso* the questions deal with the ultimate question of dogma. But in the *Purgatorio* very human things are discussed by the poet and Virgil (later with the addition of Statius, who joins them on the cornice of avarice). Aside from doctrinal questions, we touch upon historical, philosophical, and even literary matters. I think the literary comments have special interest: Dante's definition of his own "sweet new style" in Canto XXIV, for example, or the remarks on criticism in Canto XXVI.

Such discussions do not impede the narrative but rather enrich it. For gradually it is the deepening and broadening of the seer's perception which engages more and more of our attention.

Yet another facet is brought out in the *Paradiso*. As Dante, under the guidance of Beatrice, is borne upward from sphere to sphere, there are characters he meets on the way and some of them as memorable as those of the *Inferno:* the gentle Piccarda, from whom Dante learns the basic law of Heaven—and Earth too for the illuminated: that "in His will is our peace"; the affectionate Charles Martel, who gives Dante lessons on social and political science; and the complacent Cunizza, whose sins were greater and more numerous than those of

Francesca, but who has lived to repent of them and so, in a sense, to glory in them. Sharply drawn, too, is the wonderful old reactionary Cacciaguida, Dante's ancestor and as arrogant a partisan as Farinata but sanctified by his Crusader's death. To be sure there is something static about these souls as compared with the damned and the penitent, for the saints have no rebellion in them and no further need for effort, yet they come clear in all their humanity. But Heaven is above all the place where Dante probes deeper into ever more difficult mysteries, many of them specifically of dogmatic nature, such as the great doctrine of redemption or the impenetrable one of God's predestination, but some that are more than merely dogmatic, such as the search for the ultimate significance of justice in the heaven of Jupiter. Dante himself takes us more into his confidence: he tells us of his labors on the poem, "which have made him lean," of his hopes—never to be realized—of being readmitted to his beloved city; he makes us feel with him the bitterness of exile as he allows us to hear Cacciaguida's prophecy of dark and lonely years to come.

So Dante is much in the foreground, as he was in the *Purgatorio*. Yet there is a new area too in the fusion of light and contemplation. The center of our attention has shifted a little from the humanity of the characters, even from the personal revelations of Dante, to the contemplation of the ultimate—perhaps it is not too much to say: to ourselves in the face of the infinite.

The *Paradiso* is in one way very different from the first two main divisions. Dante is at great pains—always within the frame of his fiction—to persuade us that he has really been in Hell and Purgatory. But in the first canto of the *Paradiso* the poet confesses that he does not know whether his celestial journey was undertaken in the body or out of the body. He is furthermore greatly concerned to show us that the physical laws we are used to here below do not obtain in Heaven. In the first canto Beatrice tells him that the unhampered soul naturally rises—just as naturally as on earth things fall. At the end of the *Paradiso*, when Dante gazes on the Heavenly Rose, we are told that no earthly distance could measure the vast remoteness from his point of observation on the floor of the amphitheater to the upper tiers where sit the elect, and yet he can see each one clearly and distinctly. As Purgatory is closest to our own world, so Paradise is most remote from it, is indeed inconceivable in our gross physical terms. The descriptions in the *Paradiso* are magnificent, but their recurrent splendor has not quite the same appeal as the more recognizable vignettes of the *Purgatorio*. The characteristic poetry of Heaven, I think, is elsewhere; in the mingling of light, contemplation, and inner ecstasy. Here, for example, is Beatrice's homily on the tendency of the soul to rise:

> All things that be have order
> Among themselves; 'tis this that is the form
> Which makes the universe like unto God.
> And here the loftier creatures see the stamp
> Of the eternal Worth which is the goal
> For which the norm aforesaid was designed.
> Under this order things of every kind
> Do all incline, each following its lot,
> Nearer or less near to their Principle.
> Whence over the great sea of being they move on
> To divers ports, and each one is endowed
> With instinct apt to bear it on its way.
>
> (*Par.* I, 103–114)

Or better still—and this is truly heavenly verse of the sort no other poet has ever attained—when the enraptured but always articulate Dante describes his arrival in the ultimate and true heaven. It is Beatrice who tells him that they have passed from the *primum mobile* to the Empyrean:

> She spoke: "From out the greatest body we
> Have come into the heaven of pure light,
> Light of the intellect replete with love,

> Love of true good with gladness overflowing,
> Such gladness as surpasses every sweet."
>
> (*Par.* XXX, 38–42)

Yet another special beauty of the *Paradiso* for the reader who has come this far is in seeing the pattern take final form. The *Paradiso* builds on what has gone before and serves to link the work together and bring it to final completion. We see the Empress Constance in the sphere of the moon and we recall that we met her son, the great Emperor, among the heretics in Hell, and her grandson, the handsome Manfred, wandering on the hillside of Purgatory awaiting the time to begin his purgation. Theologically this opens our minds to a consideration of God's predestination, artistically it serves to keep the whole *Comedy* present with us as we draw near to the climax. The appearance of Folquet de Marseille, the troubadour bishop, in the heaven of Venus, reminds us of his fellow Provençal singers, Arnaut Daniel in the refining fire of Purgatory and Bertran de Born mutilated among the sowers of discord in Hell. The prophecies concerning Dante's own future, which he has heard fragmentarily and obscurely as he toiled through the circles of the damned or up the terraces of the Holy Mountain, are made painfully clear in the predictions of Cacciaguida. The concept of Judgment Day, which had been the despair of the damned and the hope of the penitents, is seen in all its happier and glorious significance in the final cantos of the *Paradiso*. The intercession of the Virgin, which permits Dante to enjoy the final vision, reminds us of her intercession, described by Virgil in Canto II of the *Inferno*, by which she had initiated the operations necessary for his rescue.

Now if the poem is impressive in totality, it is nothing short of entrancing in detail. It is, as has been said before, like a vast edifice built of bricks, and each individual brick has its own polish and beauty. The *terza rima*—triple rhyme—which Dante used is the only technique which would have made this possible. Its advantage is that in three lines one can express a unit of thought or a descriptive element in such a way that it can stand on its own and be complete in itself, while at the same time the middle verse of one terzina rhyming with the first and third verses of the succeeding unites the first block with the second, cements the bricks as it were, and so each brick preserves its own integrity and yet is part of the whole.

Dante is also very resourceful in his use of rhetorical and poetic devices, from simple assonance and alliteration to subtle metaphor; of all, the simile is by far his favorite and characteristic figure. The most recent census gives us some eight hundred examples; they range from the naturalistic to the bookish, the humble to the sublime. There are naturalistic similes that make us, as Eliot says, "see what the poet sees," empathetic similes that enable us to share in his responses to shock, delight, or amazement, and sublime similes that serve as an X ray to reveal the transcendental substance of his message. There are too the standard devices of the Middle Ages—catalogues, digressions, and the like, but always tactfully placed and tastefully proportioned, and there are subtleties of imagery and allusions to delight the most advanced twentieth-century perception.

Such then is the appeal of the poem as a work of art, a poetic fiction of sturdy substance and seductive ornament. And I have tried, I don't know how successfully, to suggest how the allegory is built into it. Dante's own explicitly stated allegory, I mean, the portrayal of the condition of souls in this world: the perverted or obsessed wretches who have lost the good life, those who have had a glimpse of it and strive to attain it, and those who have achieved serenity and blessedness. But the allegory may be read in other ways too. Very commonly it is interpreted as the human soul's, anyone's, Everyman's, examination of conscience, resolution of will, and eventual arrival at a state of grace. And conventionally the action is thought of as Everyman (Dante) contemplating sin and its consequences under the guidance and with the assistance of Reason (Virgil) illuminated by Faith (Statius), going on to meet Revelation (Beatrice), which opens new realms of ecstatic contemplation and ultimate satisfaction. More personally the story can be read as the poet's own "conversion"—either from philosophical error or moral divagation—and subsequent salvation through the study of the writings of virtuous pagan and Christian authorities, culminating in the ecstasy of his ultimately consoling vision. These various allegories blend and fuse with the story itself so that at the end the reader looks back with a new and deeper vision of the world the poet has created for him, aware of its implications and its ambiguities and certainly, I would think, awed by the purely creative achievement of Dante Alighieri. He has, we can see, set before us a whole world, a world of individuals, sinners, strivers, and saints, each one judged, assayed, categorized, fitted into a definite place in a firm philosophical pattern, and thereto assigned by unshakable moral values. This of course might have been done by any philosopher-scholar with a moral code and an orderly mind. But in addition to all this the characters portrayed are not merely items pouring out of a vast and infallible IBM machine; they are real people, humanly considered and warmly presented, disposed by philosophical order if you will but clothed in passion and the blood and bones of humanity. This is a miracle, I think, and it is not surprising that to Dante's simple title for his work, "the *Comedy*," his readers have prefixed the adjective *Divine*.

3

Citizen Dante

૭∾

I should like to begin with three quotations; they will, I hope, serve to indicate the direction of my argument here and perhaps also to sharpen it a little. The first is from the *Divine Comedy*. We are in Paradise, where the ultimate truths are revealed, and we are in the third heaven of that realm, the sphere of Venus, where, appropriately, truly loving souls disclose themselves to Dante. Among them is the young prince of Naples, Charles Martel, whom Dante had known briefly on the occasion of the Prince's visit to Florence in 1294. Dante had expected, it would seem, some patronage from Charles, the heir to the Neapolitan throne, and the Prince's untimely death, frustrating our poet's hopes, had also caused him to meditate on the mysteries of heredity. For while Charles was, in Dante's opinion, an admirable person, his brother, Robert, who had succeeded to the kingship, was not a man to be compared to his father Charles II. Why *is* it that inept princes so often succeed their competent sires? Why is it that incompetent or even bad sons spring from noble and virtuous parents? And Charles, beginning his rather tortuous explanation, says to Dante:

> *Or dì: sarebbe il peggio*
> *per l'uomo in terra se non fosse cive?*

and Dante answers:

"Sì," rispuos' io, "e qui ragion non cheggio."
(*Par.* VIII, 115–117)

("Say now, would it not be worse/ For man on earth were he no citizen?"/ "Yes," I replied, "I ask no reason here.")

In other words: is not society useful to man? Is not man in fact capable of developing his potential *only* in society? And Dante's answer in brief: "Of course: everyone knows that; you need cite no authority." To be sure, Dante could have cited a very good one, but my point here is not the source of his conviction but its firmness.

The second quotation is from the works of a very great poet who was Dante's contemporary but whom, for reasons I suspect not entirely unconnected with my thesis here, Dante never mentions. It is the Franciscan, Jacopone da Todi, and it goes as follows:

> Lord, of your courtesy
> Send me infirmity.
> Send me the quartan fever
> The chronic and the tertiary
> Send me the daily double sweat
> And great dropsy.
> May I have aching teeth
> Throbbing head and stomach pains
> And quinsy for my throat.[1]

This voices a fairly standard medieval motif, with long and honorable ancestry, illustrating a kind of ferocious monastic asceticism, in which in order to exalt the spirit the flesh is despised and rejected.

And somewhat similar if more gentle is the mood expressed in my third quotation from the pen of Francesco Petrarca, written only some twenty-five years, probably, after the death of Dante:

I have sought ever ways of solitude
As brooks and heath and coppice know full well,
Seeking to flee those blunted minds and fell
That would my hope of winning heaven preclude . . .[2]

Quotations two and three then depict very widespread attitudes of the medieval mind as well as exemplify certain conventional literary currents. In effect, two types of escape, one fierce, mystic, clerical, the other gentle and poetic. My point is that neither of them appears to any noticeable degree in the works of Dante Alighieri.

Let us now, against the background of our quotations, reflect on the life and works of the poet. Let us recall that he claimed for himself a noble ancestry through his father, who, to the best of our information, was a man of no great prominence. What we know of Dante's youth is largely what he chooses to tell us, usually in an oblique and ambiguous form, in the pages of his first work, *La vita nuova*, and here and there, fragmentarily, in his other works. He was early attracted to the study of literature, following the conventions of the lyric poetry of his day; he corresponded with other young poets; he fell in love with Beatrice Portinari, who died in 1290 as the poet's young manhood came to an end. He seems to have led the normal life of a Florentine youth of his class. He fought for his city against the Aretines at Campaldino (1289). Whether his marriage to Gemma Donati, whose name was more illustrious than his own in Florentine annals, preceded the death of Beatrice or not we cannot be sure. Nor do we know whether it was the death of Beatrice, as Boccaccio argues, that made him turn to the active life as a refuge from melancholy; we do know that after her death he became interested in politics and served his city in various capacities, as ambassador, as a member of the Council—Board of Aldermen as we might now call it—and ultimately as one of the two priors in the fateful summer months of 1300. His party was the Guelph, normally thought of as the papal as against the imperial Ghibelline faction; when the Guelphs, who had had Florence to themselves after the victory of Charles of Anjou over Manfred in 1266, later split into two groups, Dante became a White Guelph, ideologically very close to the imperial sympathies of the old Ghibellines, with whom in later years he came to have somewhat close rapport. Because he had taken a stand against the French and papal intervention in the affairs of his city, our poet was exiled; the injustice of his sentence, which was never rescinded, galled him deeply, and he never forgave his fellow citizens. He was however to achieve prominence in Northern Italy as a philosopher and scholar, and, one may assume, to a certain extent as a diplomat; he wandered during the years of his exile from court to court, serving as ambassador and it may be as adviser to various Italian lords, eagerly awaiting the return of imperial power to Italy, a return which would, he was sure, reduce stubborn and presumptuous Florence to obedience and permit him to come back into "the fair sheep fold where he had slept while yet a lamb." His hopes were dashed by the death of Henry VII in 1313, and he lived out the remaining eight years of his life in the courts of Verona and Ravenna.

As an obituary or editorial comment on Dante we may quote the words of the chronicler Giovanni Villani:

> Although a layman, he was well versed in almost every science; he was a supreme poet and philosopher and a perfect rhetorician; most noble both in writing and versifying and in making speeches; a supreme composer in rhyme, having the most beautiful style there ever was in our language up to his time and after . . . This Dante, because of his knowledge, was somewhat overbearing, aloof and haughty, and like a philosopher, lacking in social graces; he did not know how to converse easily with laymen; but because of his other virtues and his knowledge and the worthiness of such a fellow citizen it seems proper

to give him perpetual memory in this our *Chronicle*, even though his own noble works, which he has left us in writing, bear witness to him and bring honorable renown to our city.[3]

The simple record of Dante's rôle—a leader in his community, a vigorous partisan, adviser to lords and princes, occasionally ambassador and occasionally, by the vicissitudes of exile, a beggar—indicates a life full of toil and activity. But of course it is his writings over these troubled and busy years that hold our chief interest. Chronologically the first among them is the *Vita nuova*, which tells the story of Dante's love for Beatrice, their first meeting at the age of nine, his growing devotion to her, the joy in her greeting, the melancholy when it was withdrawn, and eventually his decision to find his happiness merely in praising her; then, her death and his resolution to prepare a work worthy of her memory. In the long history of the medieval love-cult the *Vita nuova* holds a climactic place; but, quite aside from the satisfaction it may give to historians of literature, it delights us today with its air of tenderness and innocence, although stylistically it is in fact highly sophisticated and shows the hand of a masterly technician. Original too is the form, with its mixture of prose and poetry, for the narrative is interspersed with sonnets and *canzoni*, some of them predating the composition of the work and, critics suspect, even at first intended for young ladies other than Beatrice, "a young man's fancy" being what it is.

The *Convivio*, somewhat more difficult to date although Dante's own statement indicates that it was begun some time after he had gone into exile, is a very different thing. Here too, to be sure, verse alternates with prose, but the verse, of a very different character from that of the *Vita nuova*, is quite submerged in the commentary. For here it is not Dante the lover that we see before us but Dante the philosopher, no less idealistic perhaps than the lover, but certainly less graceful, less appealing, as he is willfully more erudite and more demanding. In one sense the work is another of those vast summaries not uncommon in the medieval canon, patently didactic in purpose and encyclopedic in character. We shall come back to it for useful reinforcement of our main argument; in passing we may note that it differs from other works of Dante in that the sense of proportion, such a striking feature of the *Comedy*, for example, is almost totally absent; the second tractate is twice as long as the first, the third twice as long as the second, the fourth twice as long as the third; one shudders at the thought of the sheer bulk had Dante carried through with his design of fifteen tractates. Fortunately he broke it off—one suspects because he found that he could convey his message more artistically as well as more economically in the *Comedy*. Yet the *Convivio* has many precious passages, including those where Dante speaks with simple directness about his exile and his ambitions and the rôle of the Italian language in his life.

The Italian language indeed is the subject of another one of his works, the *De vulgari eloquentia*, written in Latin and something of a pioneer work in the field of linguistics. In successive chapters Dante sets forth his theory of the origins of speech, the great linguistic families insofar as they were known to him, and then, striving desperately to be objective, and all but unaware of his own Florentine prejudices, attempts to find the true Italian vernacular among the multitudinous dialects of fourteenth-century Italy. We may say that as the *Vita nuova* has revealed the lover, the *Convivio* the philosopher, so the *De vulgari eloquentia* shows us the scholar. A last facet of his genius is apparent in the *De monarchia*, which shows us the political scientist or, if you will, the partisan. This work, also written in Latin, consists of three major divisions, the first making the point that the world needs one monarch and no more (a central world government, as we would put it in twentieth-century terms), the second proves, at least to the author's satisfaction, that this supreme temporal ruler should be a Roman emperor, and the third chapter, which is the purely partisan one, argues that the temporal power of such a ruler is supreme in its sphere and not to be thought of as subject to the admittedly more sacred spiritual authority of the papacy.

All of the interests that are set forth in these so-called minor works, one might say all of the Dantesque personalities that are revealed in them, are fused in the *Divine Comedy*. It is Beatrice, the idealized love of the poet's youth or *Vita nuova*, who sets the action of the great poem in motion. *I' son Beatrice che ti faccio andare* (I am Beatrice who bids you go), she says, speeding Virgil to the rescue of her beleaguered lover. The philosopher is apparent in the general tone of the *Comedy* which touches, as did the *Convivio*, on all aspects of human life, ranging from the purely scientific to the metaphysical; the scholar weaves in and out, giving us instruction on such varied matters as spots on the moon, the habits of ants, or why modern, that is, Dante's, poetry is superior to that of an earlier generation. And the partisan too is never far from our company, insisting on the need for strong government, deploring the corruption of the papacy, and pressing the imperial cause up to the very highest court of Heaven itself.

In the fusion of these multiple aspects there emerges yet another, and that one is of course the truly immortal Dante, to wit, Dante the poet. It is this which adorns, deepens, and eternalizes all the rest. Without attempting any original definition of poetry or indeed calling on any ancient authority to support me here I shall content myself with the confession that to me poetry signifies an additional dimension which the poet's intuition lends to truth. We are continually aware of this dimension as we read the *Comedy*.

Lover, philosopher, scholar, partisan, and sublimely poet: this is a rare, not to say unique, combination. It is hard to think of any rival, any figure in literature, politics, or philosophy for whom a similar versatility may be claimed. Scant wonder then that Dante has received over the centuries such consistent acclaim from the sensitive, such persistent attention from the erudite.

From historical investigation to esthetic commentary, from the meticulous searching out of local references to broad considerations of style and structure in the *Comedy*, from narrow philological research to daring and alarming disquisitions on the "secret message" of the poem, criticism of Dante, which began shortly after his death and shows no sign of abating, has ranged far and wide. The present generation has been particularly interested in the *sovrasenso* or semi-mystical, religious, and metaphysical aspect of his *Comedy*, as befits a time when the esoteric and the suprarational, or, as the case may be, contrarational seems to flourish in all the arts. I risk a little being against the current of my times in what I am about to say, for, with all due respect to the investigators of the "fourth sense" and of Dante's debt to the mystics and the like (and such studies have assuredly illuminated the poem for us), I am inclined to think we still read him and will always read him for his concern with our own earth rather than his celestial raptures, for his immersion in his own times, which paradoxically eternalizes him, rather than for his supermundane interests, which remain, paradoxically again, essentially medieval. At any rate that is my thesis here. And in looking more closely at Dante's works, which I have outlined in summary form, I intend to stress his burning desire, as a man of letters, for communication, and his consuming passion, as a man *tout court*, for participation.

I believe the simple record of his life demonstrates his participant bent; this drive came out in his writings as a desire to instruct and—why not say it?—to indoctrinate. And for these ends communication was the necessary means. I shall henceforth assume that the desire to communicate, instruct, and participate are associated and born essentially of one motivation, and attempt to show how, with varying approaches, this motivation runs through the work of our poet. And then I shall say something of the substance of Dante's views, political and social, as revealed in his more overt affirmations.

Let us, with this in mind, take another and closer look at some of the minor works.

Consider for a moment the *Vita nuova*. Here, as we have seen, we have no thesis to impart, no didactic philosophy to expound, merely the tale of a bashful lover, told in whispers and, one would swear, hardly meant to be overheard. Our contemporary poet Salvatore Quasimodo[4] speaks of the "hermetic" character of Dante's youthful poems, having in mind precisely those which appear in the *Vita nuova* and using the term "hermetic," dear to the poets of his generation, to mean, as it means for them, a message so personal as to be obscure, nay almost willfully obscure. Your true hermetic invents his own language, suffers his private agonies, creates his own music, and all but challenges you to discover his secret. His appeal—and it is the appeal of most moderns, as it was for a certain strain among medieval singers—is to the élite, not the multitude. We shall not deny the implied statement of Italy's Nobel-Prize-winning poet that a certain hermeticism is perceptible in the *Vita nuova*. True. But it is the other thrust in Dante's psyche which we would stress here. And we shall note that throughout this little book the poet is never unaware of his audience. His first sonnet, he tells us, was sent abroad to invite the comments of his fellow poets. Almost every poem in the work is followed by a little exposition in prose of what the poet had meant to say in his verse. (We could often wish for similar consideration from twentieth-century poets!) And there occurs toward the end of the little book a scene which charmingly and unselfconsciously indicates Dante's concern with the public. Sometime after the death of Beatrice he wrote as follows:

> After this tribulation it came to pass at that season when many people go to behold the blessed image that Jesus

Christ hath left us for ensample of his most beautiful countenance, which my lady now beholdeth in glory, that some pilgrims passed by a way, which is almost in the middle of the city where the most gentle lady was born, lived and died; and they went, as it seemed to me, very pensively. Wherefore thinking on them, I said within myself: These pilgrims seem to me to be from a far country and I believe that they have not even heard speak of my lady and know naught of her; rather their thoughts are of other things than of these here; for perchance they are thinking of their distant friends whom we know not. Then said I within myself: I know that if these were from a near country they would appear in some wise troubled on passing through the dolorous city. Then said I within myself: If I could detain them awhile, I would make them too weep ere they issued from this city because I would say words that should make whosoever heard them, weep.[5]

This deepseated instinct to make the world a sharer in his grief, or his preoccupations, this realization of the bond which unites the individual and the community, giving purpose to the personal—all this, no matter how one phrases it, represents a desire to communicate and eventually to instruct which is at the opposite pole from the hermetic and which is I believe the truly motivating element in Dante's art. It is the measure of the strength of this need within him that we find such evidence of it in a book the nature of which is essentially private, aristocratic, and all but confessional.

More overtly than elsewhere does this public intention come out in the *Convivio*. And this in various ways. First of all it is explicitly what the *Vita nuova* is not: a work of straightforward didactic purpose. Beginning with an appeal to Aristotle's dictum that all men desire to know, Dante tells us expressly that he is writing this work for those in whom that desire is strong but who are impeded by civic and family concerns which deny them the leisure to apply themselves to the pursuit of knowledge, and for those who live at some distance from centers of study and so have not the opportunity to satisfy this natural need. Dante in effect defines himself as what we should now style a popularizer, for he does not claim himself to be a great philosopher or, as he puts it, "one who sits at the table where the bread of angels is consumed," but rather a humble student of wisdom, anxious to share what he has learned.

In order to reassure us about his credentials, he asserts that he is no longer the youthful lover who penned the *Vita nuova*, suitable perhaps to the age in which he wrote it, but a man of experience and dignity, as he intends to show by the use, among other devices, of a somewhat abstruse style. If he does not actually repudiate the *Vita nuova*, at least he recreates his own literary personality; the intimate and the confessional are cast aside and he proclaims himself openly as teacher and guide, seeking not merely to find but also patently to instruct an audience. And instruction, in truth, the readers of the *Convivio* will have aplenty. Broadly speaking we may find in the work two different kinds of instruction; one simply informational, as for example the exposition on the Heavens, the movements of the planets, the choirs of angels and the like; the other moral or directional, for Dante lays down a number of rules for the conduct of life. And the point I want to bring out is that, although he professes to admire the life of contemplation, his directives, for we must call them that, apply always to man in society and indeed assume a social relationship as a point of departure for a code of behavior. Consider, for example, what he has to tell us concerning the ages of man and the virtues appropriate to each age. This is one of the most characteristic as it is one of the most beautiful pages of the *Convivio*, and I should like to quote again directly from the author. Of *youth*, which according to Dante lasts up to the twenty-fifth year, he says that four things are necessary to that age: obedience, sweetness, sensitiveness to shame, grace of body; and of obedience he says, "You are to know then that like as he who was never in a city would not know how to keep the way without instruction from him who has frequented it, so the adolescent who enters into the deceitful (*erronea*) wood of this life would not know how to keep to the right path if it were not shown him by his elders. And their instructions would be of no use if he were not obedient to their commandments." [6] It is interesting and perhaps not irrelevant here to note how this hypothetical youth begins his journey in a forest, here *erronea* as the pilgrim of the *Comedy* will find it *oscura*, and how the proper goal of a traveller seems to be a city, even as Beatrice (*Par.* xxx, 130) will proudly define the Empyrean as *la nostra città*.

For *manhood*, the prime of life, he lays down the necessary virtues as temperance, bravery, love, courtesy, and loyalty; civic virtues all; indeed Dante exemplifies them not by reference to the saints or philosophers but by reference to Aeneas the hero or man of action. Similarly for *age* our poet prescribes prudence, justice, generosity, and affability; only for the last state of all, decrepitude, does he suggest that we "lower the sails of our worldly activities and turn to God with all our purpose and heart; so that we may come into that port with all sweetness and peace." [7]

We need not linger on the pedagogical intent of the *De vulgari eloquentia*, written, as Dante loftily informs us, "to enlighten the discernment of those who walk through the streets like blind men, generally fancying that those things that are in front of them are behind them," nor on the *De monarchia*, which has a definite political thesis to expound. One is disquisitional in character, the other polemic, but both are didactic and reinforce the image of Dante the social-conscious poet, not merely aware of his public but eager to direct it. And as we approach the *Comedy* we shall not dwell so much on further evidences of this missionary drive, which are numerous and apparent to all, but we shall alter somewhat the direction of our enquiry and, holding it now proved that Dante is profoundly interested in society and its destiny, ask rather what prescription does he give us. We have seen enough, in other words, to establish his social interests; we may now ask what suggestions he offers in his climactic poem for a world which was in fact, and must have seemed to him in his bitter exile even more so, chaotic and directionless. But before getting to the second phase of our study I cannot resist illustrating Dante's frankness in advertising his mission, legible, for those who care to read it, in the very first terzina of the *Comedy*. *Nel mezzo del cammin di nostra vita/ Mi ritrovai per una selva oscura/ Chè la diritta via era smarrita* (Midway along the journey of our life/ I found myself within a gloomy wood/ For the right pathway had been lost to view). A simple declarative sentence. But observe the shift in pronouns. The main verb is in the first person singular: *I found myself*, but the modifying phrase contains the plural possessive: in the midst of *our* life. *We* are in it with Dante, or he is sharing his lot with us, whichever way you choose to put it. Is it then too much to assume that the last line, "Because the right way was lost," applies as much to us; that is, to Dante's contemporary society, as to the poet's personal plight? I do not think so, especially since Marco Lombardo in the *Purgatorio* uses a similar phrase in speaking to Dante, but employs the collective plural to signify that Dante *and* his contemporaries had departed from the right road: *se'l mondo presente disvia in voi è la cagione*; "If the present world goes off the road—in you (you all) is the cause" (*Purg.* xvi, 82–83). And of the two examples of earlier transmundane travellers Dante cites in the *Inferno* one is St. Paul, symbolizing surely the spiritual discoveries that our poet is going to make for us, and the other our old friend Aeneas, whose journey was justified for the good it might do the Empire, that is, organized temporal society.

It is indicative, by the way, of the essential social nature of Dante's genius that the pilgrimage of the poet through the kingdoms of the other world is not undertaken alone: Virgil accompanies him through Hell and Purgatory and Beatrice through the successive spheres of Heaven. Only in the very last canto is Dante truly on his own and even there only after an introduction by St. Bernard. His exposition throughout the whole *Comedy* springs out of conversation and is rarely a matter of straightforward "lecturing." Aside from being an artistic merit, this pattern reveals, I think, the essence of Dante's inner nature. And—another brief tangent—lest anyone think that Dante wrote his comedy primarily for his own satisfaction and not for your good and mine, let him but note the solemn instructions given him by Beatrice and Cacciaguida, both of whom make it clear that the poet has been given not a private vision but one to be shared with his fellow men in "this life which is but a race to death."

But let us now see what Dante has to offer. He is concerned with both ethics and government, which is to say, matters of behavior and matters of legislation. He does not always keep these concepts separate in the course of his instructional exposition. As a Florentine, and indeed as one who had taken part in the government of the city, he is interested in the destiny of his native town and naturally troubled by the factionalism that was rampant in his time. But his prescription is more moral than technical; he is closer to Savonarola than to Machiavelli. He inquires of Ciacco in the sixth Canto of the *Inferno* what can be the reason for the continual dissension in the city, and receives the answer that its source is in envy and greed and not, as a professor of political science might have observed, the result of the failure to set up a form of government that would be sufficiently strong and given long enough term in power to deal with predictable and often minor dissensions. Later, when more illustrious and able statesmen put the same question to him, Dante gives the answer that the reason for Florence's unstable condition is *La gente nuova e i subiti guadagni,* "the new people and quickly-made wealth" (*Inf.* XVI, 73); or, in modern terms, "all those immigrants and too much money for their own good"—again a diagnosis as much moral as political.

These convictions are more positively set forth in the central cantos of the *Paradiso* where Dante meets his ancestor Cacciaguida. This noble old Crusader had dwelt in Florence before the corruption of wealth and the adulteration of the primitive stock had done their foul work. With Dante listening in reverent approval, the old warrior describes twelfth-century Florence as peaceful, sober and chaste, and pure in stock. Here very specifically it is stated that the immigration (from such "foreign" centers as Certaldo, some twenty miles away) has corrupted the blood and hence the virtues of the Florentines. Dante's prescription for his city need not of course be identical with his notions for broader political units. In truth what he has to say of Florence is not in nature very different from what many an older citizen might have to say today about Boston or Philadelphia. His reflections are sentimental rather than philosophical. But on the larger issues of government he is not silent either. Again let us begin by looking at the negative side. In the conversation with Marco Lombardo, to which we have made passing reference, Dante poses a question which in essence is more philosophical than political: granting, as Marco had propounded, that the pursuit of virtue is all but neglected nowadays and the world is in decay, is the cause of this to be sought in nature or in the stars? Marco's reply turns the question in a political direction. Stressing the necessity of free will, Marco goes on in a passage so beautiful that I am reluctant to summarize or paraphrase:

> "Out from the hand of Him who holds it dear
> Ere it have being—like a little maid
> In childlike fickleness twixt smiles and tears—
> The simple soul comes forth, and nothing knows
> Save that, as from a joyous Maker sent,
> It blithely turns to what affords delight.
> Of lesser good it savors first the taste,
> Wherewith deceived it falls to swift pursuit
> If guide or check divert not this first love.
> Hence was law needful to apply the rein,
> And needful was a king who might discern

> At least the towers of truth's citadel.
> And laws there are but who turns hand to them?
> None, for the pastor who walks on ahead
> May ruminate but has no cloven hoof."
>
> (*Purg.* XVI, 85–99)

In other words Dante's diagnosis is quite simple: the world needs a temporal ruler; the papacy has cast down the Emperor and attempted to usurp his powers; a simple reinstatement of imperial authority would set things right. And I would have you note how a moral question is given a political answer, how, as it were, Heaven is brought down to earth.

And what of the affirmative side; what are things when they are right? We may find Dante's answer put most clearly and persuasively in the fourth tractate of the *Convivio*, where, as elsewhere in his works, he states his case for world government:

> "And as an individual man requires the companionship of home and household for his completeness, so likewise a household requires a district for its completeness, since otherwise it would suffer many defects which would be a hindrance to felicity. And since a district cannot satisfy itself in everything, needs must there be a city for its satisfaction. And further the city requires for its arts and for its defence to have mutual relations and brotherhood with the neighbouring cities; wherefore the kingdom was instituted. And inasmuch as the human mind rests not in the limited possession of land, but ever, as we see by experience, desires to acquire more territory, needs must discords and wars arise betwixt kingdom and kingdom. Which things are the tribulations of cities, and through the cities of districts, and through the districts of households, and through the households of man; and thus is felicity impeded. Wherefore to abolish these wars and their causes, needs must all the earth and whatsoever is given to the generations of men for a possession, be a monarchy, that is one single princedom having one prince; who, possessing

all things and not being able to desire more, shall keep the kings contented within the boundaries of their kingdoms, so that there shall be peace between them, in which peace the cities may have rest, and in this rest the districts may love one another, and in this love the households may receive whatsoever they need, and when they have received this, man may love in felicity, which is that whereto man was born." [8]

To Dante it seems quite simple then to demonstrate that the world needs one central government, and that a strong one, if there is to be an end to regional and national rivalries, which by their repeated calls to arms make the attainment of peace impossible. I do not think that we of the twentieth century are in a position to dispute his major thesis. If, however, we have universal peace, many of the problems that beset governments nowadays become irrelevant. So we must not be disappointed if we find in Dante no discussion of checks and balances, parliamentary procedure, the rôle of the opposition, and the like. It was natural and indeed inevitable in the Balkanized society of the late Middle Ages to think of the function of government as primarily one of keeping order, and if that can be solved from the top and hierarchically cleared through the lower echelons, as Dante argues that it can be, then "government" is essentially a police force administered by incorruptible men—princes, Dante would have them. All we need is a clear warrant of authority, fortunately readily available, given the legitimate primacy of the Emperor. A concept simple, austere, and fundamentally aristocratic. Perhaps it might work; it should be said that it has worked remarkably well in certain large areas at certain times; in imperial Rome, in China, and perhaps for a while in the Russia of the Czars.

Yet Dante's theories are not entirely consistent. For one thing his own experience in politics had been in a republic, more oligarchic than democratic to be sure, but a republic nevertheless, where office was held not by heredity but by election. Indeed, the Florentines had specifically excluded the aristocracy from participation in government and, in order to make himself eligible for office, Dante, regardless of whether or not his claim to noble birth was valid, had to enroll in a guild of artisans. And if the republic was split by factions, still it worked better than any other system with which Dante came in contact; certainly it was a political reality, while the Empire remained, at least in Italy, merely a concept. And in justice to the Florentines, in whom their talented and embittered compatriot saw so many flaws, moral no less than political, their spirit and their unity, made effective through a recurrently instable but vigorously democratic constitution, were sufficient not only to withstand the Emperor but even to break his power. It may be that Dante's awareness of the hard facts of political life as well as certain theories of a theological nature led him to return again and again to a consideration of what is essentially a basic flaw in the hierarchical concept. If we are to have hereditary princes, the success of the system—by Dante's own definition of success, which is to say, the maintenance of peace and order—must depend on the virtue of the hereditary officers, "virtue" here being understandable either in the Christian or the Machiavellian sense. But in fact virtue, in either sense, is all too obviously something which is *not* inherited. The theme of the decay of the aristocracy is a recurrent one in all Dante's writings; most bitterly expressed perhaps in the fourteenth canto of the *Purgatorio* where, in discussing the great families of Romagna, Guido del Duca, an aristocrat of that region, remarks with melancholy that of the old first families the happiest are those that have no heirs, since in all cases where a son survives he is unworthy of his father. The entire fourth book of the *Convivio* is dedicated to the proposition that virtue is *not* a matter of heredity, and Dante has things to say that sound almost revolutionary against the background of feudalism; indeed, he specifically contradicts the definition of nobility attributed to Frederick II, the great Emperor whom Dante truly admired. For the Emperor had defined an essential of nobility as "ancient riches," or as we

would say, inherited wealth, and Dante attacked both elements of the definition. In truth, he says, the man of noble
ancestry who is unworthy of his name is properly to be held
inferior to all, since he has neglected the example set before
him. "And thus he who is ennobled in race, by his father or
some forebear, and perseveres not therein, is not only base but
basest, and worthy of all scorn and vituperation, more than
any other churl." [9] Yet, if we follow Dante in the further development of this theme, we may have some sympathy for the
degenerate bearer of an illustrious name, for, commenting on
the princes in the pleasant hollow of the holy mount, who
await their time to go to their purgation, Sordello informs
Dante that:

> But rarely does the virtue of mankind
> Rise through the branches: He will have it so
> Who gives it, that it may be traced to Him.
> *(Purg.* VII, 121–123)

a principle which would make the inheritance of virtue not
merely unlikely but impossible. As we follow our poet's investigation of this field one step further, in the aforementioned
conversation with Charles Martel—and we now return to the
passage which served as my point of departure—a principle
emerges which, logically honored, would certainly have considerably modified Dante's monolithic theory of government.
For here Charles pursues his basic principle that man is a social
animal and society is a necessary condition of life with the following argument:

> Therefore must the roots
> Of your effects be different, thus it is
> That one is born a Solon, Xerxes one,
> Melchisedech another and a fourth
> One who in flight aerial lost his son.
> The circling nature which to mortal wax

> Is as the seal, employs its skill aright,
> But does not take account of residence.
> (*Par.* VIII, 121–129)

Endowments then and aptitudes are not hereditary and it follows logically, as Dante (through Charles) goes on to say:

> When nature finds herself in ill accord
> With fortune, her effects are always ill—
> Like any other seed sown out of place.
> And if the world down there would but take heed
> Of the foundation nature has prepared
> And follow that it would have goodly folk.
> But you will turn to the religious life
> One born to bear a sword, and make a king
> Of one more fitted to write homilies,
> So that your track strays from the proper road.
> (*Ibid.*, 139–148)

This theory if followed out would certainly have played havoc with the medieval social order. Probably Dante intended to mean only that among the sons of rulers the first-born was not necessarily the best to succeed the father or that some princes would have made better priests. Still the concept as stated is bold and unmodified and strangely at odds with Dante's otherwise conservative principles, based on respect for inherited authority.

For after all, though his emperor was to be elected, the Electors were hereditary, and Dante would certainly have been appalled at the notion of a popular vote for the Chief Executive. And the hereditary superiority of Roman blood is proclaimed not only in the *De monarchia* but in the fifteenth canto of the *Inferno*, where Dante makes a distinction between the virtuous Florentines who, like himself, had descended from the original Roman seed and the "beasts" of Fiesole who had come down from the hills to adulterate and debase the purity of that birthright. And how openly he delights in

his own ancestry when old Cacciaguida comes forth from the
Cross of Mars to acknowledge and receive him! The plain fact
is that in his study of social and political affairs, both experience and theory suggested contrary principles; philosophically and theologically the universe must be ordered, yet salvation hinges on liberty. And alas, as Dante surveyed his
contemporary world he could see on the one hand how frequently the ideal feudalistic hierarchy was productive of injustice and chaos, while at the same time the tentative democracy of his own city had bred a factionalism which embittered
his life.

So we may say, then, as we approach a conclusion, that con-
servatives and liberals may both find support in Dante, even
as, in the field of esthetics, the champions of the classic and the
romantic, the realist and the idealist, or even for that matter
both Protestant and Catholic in the religious sphere. Dante
never got down to the actual mechanics of government; he
had strong convictions, a lot of practical and painful experience, and prophetic vision; all these were fused to be sure, but
fused poetically rather than rationally. This does not however
affect, our central argument, which is quite simply that our
poet, attaining his bliss, as he does, in mystic contemplation of
the supreme delights of the world above, knowing that world
to be the reality of which our life is but a figure, nonetheless
through all his creative career was deeply and vitally concerned about our human destiny, our practical problems of
community living, our political welfare, in a word, the here
and now.

I think he was himself aware of this commitment and of its
spiritual danger. Dante was not, like Petrarch, a man morbidly
inclined to dwell on and magnify his own inner contradictions, but that is not to say he did not have them. Let us recall
the central moment of the *Comedy*, when the poet is at last
permitted to gaze upon Beatrice, the love of his youth and
symbolic at this point of his spiritual aspirations, let us say his
better self. (There are infinite subtleties in the discussion of

Beatrice's mystic, allegorical, moral, and even ecclesiastical meaning here and elsewhere; I choose merely the simplest and I hope least polemic version.) For in truth she addresses him with the reproving voice of conscience and all but breaks his spirit with her harsh criticism of his misspent years after her death. She explains to the attendant, and—one would swear— somewhat embarrassed, angels that "When I was risen from the flesh to spirit,/ Beauty and virtue having waxed in me—/ He found me then less pleasing and less dear/ And turned his steps on ways removed from truth/ Pursuing empty images of good/ Whose idle promises are ne'er redeemed," (*Purg.* xxx, 127–132) and then, turning directly to Dante, challenges him to refute the truth of the charge—which he is of course unable to do.

Readers and scholars for centuries have wrestled with defining the true nature of Dante's infidelity: What were these "empty images of good" that he pursued? Dissipation? Pagan philosophy? Perhaps, because Beatrice is after all woman as well as symbol, another woman? Specifically we shall never know with certainty, but we do know Dante's words in answer, which come forth in a barely audible voice through penitent tears: "The things at hand/ With their false pleasure turned aside my steps/ As soon as your face was concealed from me" (*Purg.* xxxi, 34–36). "The things at hand" are, in the original, "*le presenti cose.*" Things then of this world. Of the many possible readings of this phrase, which does not exclude the concurrent validity of other interpretations, may one not see here simply Dante, the medieval Christian, well aware of the transcendent value of the eternal and conscious of his duty to fix his purpose on his soul's salvation, yet aware too of his own commitment in the transitory matters of his time, including party politics and social problems? If he aspired, as we all must, to citizenship in "that Rome where Christ is a Roman," he cherished too and, cherishing, analyzed and studied with participant passion "the threshing floor which makes us all so fierce." This passion, had he not properly repented of it, might well have stood in the way of his salvation in terms of the Christianity on which he was nourished and to which he was deeply faithful. Yet it is this passion which made him a poet and which, no matter what Beatrice may have thought of it, has assured him another kind of immortality. It is not for us to say whether Dante's soul resides, after six and one-half centuries, in the Heaven of his dreams; we do know, however, that this world of embattled and suffering, aspiring and sinful mankind, from which he could never detach himself, will not let him die.

4
Hell: Topography and Demography

ह⁣≈

Over the centuries scholars, experts, and merely humble readers of the *Comedy* have asked the question: why did Dante
write his great work? To celebrate Beatrice and establish his
reputation, as may be said of the *Vita nuova*? To give himself
a standing among intellectuals, as is, in part at least, the
avowed intent of the *Convivio*? To instruct the public on
matters of general interest, somewhat neglected by others, as is
the stated purpose of the *De vulgari eloquentia* and the *De
monarchia*? For purposes of moral and political propaganda,
evidence of which is not lacking in the *Comedy* itself? Or shall
we see in the *Comedy*, as Flamini did, part III of the poet's
autobiography, the *Vita nuova* and the *Convivio* being respectively parts I and II? Didactic, confessional, polemical—the
poem is all this in intent. But in fact it is a poem and, as such,
must have been conceived primarily as a work of art. Whatever his ultimate purpose, the poet's immediate urgency must
have been the construction of a *navicella* fit to carry the burden of his message. Neither exhortation nor instruction would
be of any avail if his public did not read the book. As the
various apostrophes to the reader indicate, scattered as they are
at discreetly arranged intervals, our poet always had his audience in mind.

Nor is there any doubt of his concern with narrative plan

and tactics. "Neither the world, nor the theologians," confesses Dorothy Sayers,[1] "nor even Charles Williams had told me the one great, obvious, glaring fact about Dante Alighieri of Florence—that he was simply the most incomparable story-teller who ever set pen to paper." It is time, perhaps, to tell the news to others or at least remind ourselves of it; if this were not the simple truth of the matter the world would not have taken him to its heart and even theologians might have found him less fascinating. It has always seemed to me that, like all good story-tellers, Dante puts forth a great and calculated effort in the first chapter of his tale in order to seize our interest and give us the initial impetus to carry through. From the story-telling point of view, the *Inferno* is the richest of the three great divisions in action, variety, characterization, and dramatic description. Here, in the words of Malagoli, "poetry finds its place suspended, as it were, between the savor of concrete things and a breath of the sublime." [2] No doubt this is a commonplace, but like all sound commonplaces it bears repeating, especially in an age—as ours seems to be—when the "theologians" or at least the anagogical explicators are so busy with "figures," symbols, and the authenticity of Dante's Thomism.

I believe, too, that the aforementioned qualities, which characterize attractive and absorbing narration, can be brought out by consideration of the physical background of the story and the individuals who stand out against it; the shape and topography of the *doloroso regno* and its *gravi cittadin*, the "concrete things" of which Malagoli speaks. Most of the allegory of the *Inferno* is inherent in the tale and not embroidered over it (as is the case with the entrance to Purgatory, or the political vision at the end of that *cantica*); most of the instruction is likewise implicit (unlike the lectures on vows, moon spots, and angelic natures in the *Paradiso*). These are things of beauty and moral utility, but I doubt whether most readers would have reached them, were it not for the immediacy and the realism of the *Inferno*; "To possess poetry

it was necessary to pass through man," says Salvatore Quasimodo of our poet,[3] and the reader, too, I think, must prepare
himself for the great illuminations of the later *cantiche* by sub-
mersion in the harsh and craggy world of the *Inferno*, vibrant
with spectacular and diversified personalities, for in truth the
characters of the *Inferno* are similar only if seen *sub specie
theologiae*; intellectually, physically, and even morally they
run through the entire human spectrum.

The configuration of Hell, in a sense, matches the design of
the other two realms. It is a kind of mirror image of Purgatory;
in the one case we have a series of descending ditches, in the
other a like pattern of ascending terraces. It is suggestive, too,
of the Rose of the Empyrean, in that, seen from the bottom, it
could well have the aspect of a vast amphitheater. Ranged
above Dante as he stands on the ice of Cocytus are the rows of
sinners (though he cannot see them), even as the serried ranks
of saints meet his eye ascending from the center of the Rose.
These symbolic similarities have their purpose, but if we turn
from symbolism to realism we shall soon see how vastly different the Infernal topography is from that of either of its sister
realms. However we may admire the formalized beauty of
Purgatory or the significant spaciousness of Heaven I think
we shall have to concede that Hell is richer in the variety of its
landscape. Indeed, this must necessarily be so even for the sake
of the allegory; for there is but one way to salvation and there
are many avenues of error. So the terraces of the way of redemption are similar, for one inspiration motivates all the penitent, and since the Blessed, as Dante tells us, really dwell in
only one heaven, the symbolic appearances they make hardly
call for differentiation save in their order. What matters to the
penitent and the saved is what they have in common: the
damned can be—indeed, must be—individualized and solitary,
and hence different.

It follows that the compartments of Hell are very sharply
divided, and passing from one to the other requires great
effort and ingenuity on the part of Dante and Virgil; on occa-

sion it is not made quite clear just how they do it. For the inmates, passage from one section to another is impossible (this law is clearly stated in *Inf.* XXIII, 55–57). In Purgatory all the terraces are connected by stairways, apparently open to all, and, once the true Purgatory has begun, relatively easy of ascent; in the symbolic Heaven the law of spiritual gravity makes the ascent easy—indeed, inevitable—and the true Heaven has no subdivisions. Leaving aside the allegory of these distinctions, we may see at once that the Inferno is of necessity less homogeneous than its sister realms and has, on the score of topographical diversity, much to offer. There are —in defiance it would seem of the basic allegory, although Dante knows how to turn it to his purpose—even occasions when the poets go up instead of down. But at this point it might be useful to remind ourselves in detail of the pattern— which is in effect also to recall to our minds the general scheme of Hell.

Topographical Hell does not begin with Canto 1 of the poem. Whatever be their thematic or structural connections, the action of the first two cantos takes place on our earth. Nor do I think the sinister portal marks the limit of the true Hell; it is a signpost but not a boundary marker. This is made clear by the nature of the souls we find just beyond it, who may not claim Infernal citizenship. Since the first circle is clearly labeled as such by Dante we may, for topographical purposes, think of the entire kingdom as encircled by the Acheron, much as the mighty ocean (in myth as in fact) encircles our living world. Apparently the only way to reach the *città dolente* is by crossing this dread river; we may visualize it, I think, as somewhat high-banked. If it were not, the simile of the falling autumn leaves would lack something in accuracy. It must be tolerably wide and deep, else there were no need of a ferryman. Once across, a somewhat surprising landscape confronts the poets and the reader. Although Dante cannot see very clearly, it is evident that he is walking not upon a craggy, descending gradient but upon a plain, and light soon appears to illuminate the path to the illustrious souls of the past. Presently, the poets approach a noble castle, which has around it all the appurtenances of a pastoral scene from the chivalrous romances. It has a *bel fiumicello,* Hell's second and often forgotten river—is it connected with the more conventional Infernal system of waterworks, one wonders? Probably not. Whatever its source, its correspondences are evocative and honorable. For as Dante will have to cross Lethe to walk with Beatrice and touch his brow to the river of grace in order to have his supreme vision, so here he must cross this little stream in order to mingle with the *spiriti magni.* Is it allegorically eloquence, as Benvenuto says—or something better? Beyond it lies a meadow of fresh green, and rising from that, the pleasant little hill (open, luminous, and high) from which Dante can survey the great shades of antiquity. It is a foretaste of both the Garden of the princes and the Earthly Paradise itself, not elaborated, but adequately outlined; the princes, to be sure, have flowers of unearthly beauty and fragrance, but even the princes do not have the castle or the river. (Hell is extremely well irrigated, no small feature of its attraction.) This oasis of virtue, this subdued but authentic pastoral, may be for the scholar (and possibly the author) a *"locus amoenus topos,"* [4] but for the reader, as for the pilgrim Dante, it is a genuine part of Hell's landscape.

Both the illumination and the spaciousness of Limbo are stressed by contrast to the circle of the lustful, where Dante takes note of the smaller scope (*men loco cinghia*) and the oppressive darkness. Of the landscape as such he says nothing; one has the impression of the sinners whipped around in a kind of void, with the poets standing on a ledge to watch them as one might watch the wheeling of birds from the brow of a cliff. If there is a plain of any extent either around them or beneath them they cannot see it; the ecstasy of lovers, however illicit, does not allow them to tread the earth. In the succeeding circle of the gluttonous, our feet are on recognizable ground again, though it is by no means firm ground, but the cold, soggy mud of a snow-swept bog. It does not seem to be a particularly extensive meadow—or swamp, for it has something of that nature—since the poets can get through it fairly rapidly, but it cannot be too small either, since, when Dante comes to (and just how he moved from the lustful to this category he does not tell us; did Virgil carry him in his swoon?) he beholds "new torments and new tormented ones" as far as his eye can see in the oppressive darkness. It is, we may say, a muddy arc of level ground leading to a downward path, which brings the travellers to the jousting place of the avaricious and prodigal.

The fourth circle gives us another plain; this time it is not sodden with rain but arid and rocky. By way of somber relief, the brooklet, "darker than perse," meets the poets as they leave the grim jousting and pours down to what Binyon calls a "fen," in which the various kinds of wrathful wallow and complain. One has the impression of a pond, choked with mud or perhaps weeds, yet sufficiently deep to require a boat for passage. It reminds us a little of the Acheron, boatman and all, and it, too, marks a frontier, setting the lower Hell off from the upper. But here we may simply note its aspect: part river, like the Acheron; part swamp, something like the mud of Ciacco's discontent, but more so, and put into sharp contrast with the dry (and sterile) setting for the avaricious. Further on comes yet another surprise—the walls of a city, beyond which Dante can discern the towers of sinister worship, even as the medieval traveller, when approaching the gates of a walled town, must have seen the spires of the churches and the public buildings looming large beyond them. There is, indeed, a good deal of contemporary detail in this passage. Describing the burial ground just inside the walls, Dante tells us that it could be compared to Aliscamps, *dove Rodano stagna*, just as, in fact, the muddy Styx lies sluggish and menacing behind them. We may note again that for all the overriding claustrophobia of Hell, which narrows as the poets descend, the perverse cemetery of the heretics is quite spacious, "a

wide, desolate campagna," as L. O. Kuhns[5] called it. It may be
remarked here that the funnel shape of Hell suggests that each
successive category of sinners is smaller in number, and
broadly speaking, this is true. At the frontier the indifferent
are countless—"I had not thought death had undone so many"
—while the very center contains only one sinner, the arch-
fiend himself. Furthermore, it seems likely that there are more
incontinent than violent, more violent than deceitful. But I am
not sure this principle holds in every detail—Dante probably
does not mean to imply that there are more simonists than
thieves, for example—and, in the descriptions of landscape
that chiefly concern us here, some of the lower *bolge*, circles,
are made to appear relatively spacious.

Comes then the pause on the brink of lower Hell, followed
by the slithering descent to the rings of the violent. This zone
has a kind of unity in its variety which is appropriate to its
quasi-autonomy as a subdivision; it is all on one level and re-
produces the general motif of the upper Hell, having again an
encircling river, a wood (it was a thicket of spirits in Limbo
but a wood for all that) and, innermost, the burning sand,
constantly rekindled by the flakes of flame. It is a microcosm
in which topographical or meteorological elements previously
encountered reappear in somewhat different combination.
(This manipulation of the familiar is a constant weapon of
Dante's art; we shall not enlarge on it here.) It is worth
noting, I think, how in this area Dante makes a special effort to
give his landscape some resemblance to our earth. The landslip
by which the poets descend to the encounter with the centaurs is like the one near Trent; the wood is strange indeed but
the Maremma comes to mind; the dikes by which the fiery
desert is traversed are not unlike those lining the Brenta. This
is a device to which Dante frequently resorts in the course of
his poem; the examples here are especially notable because
they are found in every one of the three violent circles. Here
the effect is to make us feel at once familiar with the successive
scenes and horrified at them, as of a well-known landscape

seen through dark, distorting glasses. However familiar the dikes and the Maremma and the landslide, the blood-red rivers serve to indicate that we are no longer in our world. The province of the violent is half recognizable and half unnatural, a proper setting for the venerable Brunetto (wise and erudite but no longer free to move with the solemn gravity of the sage) and the misguided Piero, loyal to his master but "towards himself unjust."

Separation, isolation, contrast: such are the principles of Hell's scheme. The circles are set off from each other as we have noted, and the larger subdivisions even more dramatically so. Between the march of Violence and the double kingdom of Fraud there is an even deeper descent than that which separates the upper realm from the outer circle of the murderers and robbers. Only by persuading the genius of Fraud himself to bear them into his abyss can the poets descend in safety (and terror) to the Malebolge.

Malebolge too has its own integrity. It is hard to speak of landscape here for the *bolge* are, in the main, too narrow to allow much scope for scenery of any kind. Yet there is plenty of diversity. In the ditches of the seducers and panders, the soothsayers and the hypocrites, the impression of very restricted space is particularly strong and we focus but little on the environment. Narrow also is the unfragrant abode of the flatterers, almost, one would suspect, the narrowest of all. On the other hand, there is a suggestion that the ghastly plain occupied by the sowers of discord must be of some extent since the multitude of mutilated figures Dante meets there is greater than could have been found in all the battlefields of strife-torn Apulia. I have the feeling—perhaps because of the reference to the Libyan sands—that the thieves also have considerable space to maneuver in. But this is only one kind of variation; we may note how Dante again mixes the elements of his *mises en scène*. We have plains, a desert, and water (or at least liquid —as in the case of the *fiumicello* of Limbo, one must wonder a little bit about the source of the barrators' pitch—is it connected with the main rivers, and if not, how does it cross them, for surely it must be a complete circle?). In a more specialized area we have a privy, a hospital, and a two-lane city street. Another intriguing variant—not strictly topographical—appears in Dante's change of direction; no less than three times he reverses his usual Infernal descent to move upward. Virgil carries him up the bank of the simonists, and helps him out of the valley of the thieves, but Dante makes quite a point (and an incidental moral allegory) of his own laborious climb up from the sixth *bolgia*. One would think there would be also some slight ascent necessary to escape from the *Malebranche* even if the bridge is broken, but Dante mentions only the precipitous toboggan ride (Virgil being the vehicle) down the outer wall into the pouch of the hypocrites.

The one element so far lacking in the wide range of physical backgrounds is supplied by the last stage of all—the ice floor of the Inferno. So looking back now that we have seen it all we can see that we have truly had everything: plains, deserts, swamps, rivers, lakes, woods, even, in essence, mountains. We have tramped under rain, hail, snow, fire, and hurricane; to be sure there has been visible no sun nor moon nor sky but there have been plenty of fiery illumination and (in Limbo) a pleasant and soothing radiance that, if not quite sunshine, is the next best thing. All of these elements have combined and separated and recombined in new patterns, sometimes unobtrusive and sometimes forced upon our attention. It is no wonder that the reader cannot lay the book down, no wonder that Coleridge could say that "the topographic reality of Dante's journey through Hell" is "one of his great charms" and "gives a striking peculiarity to his poetic power." [6]

Though perhaps it is not strictly within our province, we cannot omit a word on the second landscape of Hell: the landscape of reference. We have noted Dante's use of a scene familiar to his readers to reinforce the verisimilitude of various features of the Infernal world: the landslip near Trent, the dikes of the Brenta, to which we could add a number of others, the falls of San Benedetto, the towers of Bologna, the frozen Danube, and the like. But there is also a landscape of suggestion; the *Inferno* is punctuated with vignettes of our own earth, the effect of which is to relieve the oppressive atmosphere of Hell and incidentally to celebrate the transient but authentic beauty of our mortal habitat. I have in mind such passages as the opening of Canto xxiv, painting the first days of the "stripling year" or the evocation of summer twilight in Canto xxvi "when the fly gives way to the mosquito." Such nostalgic pictures of the world of the living are possible only in the *Inferno*; it is only Hell's "exiles of eternity" who may sigh for the "sweet light" and the "life serene." "Above in lovely Italy," Virgil may say, almost casually; in the *Purgatorio*, Sapia repudiates (as she must) her earthly citizenship, and in the *Paradiso* our world has become a mere "threshing floor." If the "brooklets" of the Casentino, which Master Adam yearns for, are not strictly speaking a part of Hell's topography, they yet serve to refresh his memory and illuminate his inner vision—and the reader's as well.

But it is time now to consider the population of these diversified zones and climates which make up the domain of the three-faced Emperor. Ernst Robert Curtius wrote some years ago that the personnel of the *Comedy* had never been adequately analyzed;[7] we can hardly hope to approach adequacy in the scope of these pages, but we may bring together a few interesting facts with attendant implications. Let us begin with some census figures.

By my count, there are 164 definitely named or easily identified characters in the *Inferno*. (I count here only residents and not figures merely alluded to.) Of these, some eighty[8] are from the classical world, four may be thought of as biblical, and the rest are largely from Dante's own contemporary society, though we must allow ourselves a little freedom in the definition of this area. The mingling of these various sects is not without its purpose. Putting together such figures as Judas on the one hand and Brutus and Cassius on the other is in line

with our poet's deliberate and self-conscious historical syncretism, the principal cultural intention of the *Comedy*, which is
sharpened here if we recall that Satan is the third element of
the group: Old Testament, New Testament, and classical be-
trayers meet at the center of the universe. But I think that in
the *Inferno* Dante is not so much concerned with the blending
of the classical and the Judeo-Christian traditions as such (this
is more marked in the *Purgatorio*, though since he cannot
bring it out in the characters of the narrative it has to be em-
phasized in the embellishment and the collateral rhetoric) as
with blending antiquity and the present into one homogeneous family of man. It has been frequently observed, in this
connection, that Dante creates his own "exemplary figures";
characters such as Francesca and Ugolino have all the eternal
mythopoeic virtue of any character from Homer or Sophocles. It is less commonly noted that his strategy has both fronts
in mind: Ulysses, Jason, and Alexander mingle, not unobtrusively perhaps, but in a quite familiar fashion, with sly plotters
from Romagna, Bolognese seducers, or petty Italian tyrants.
Dante's own familiarity with Virgil has a unique immediacy
and spontaneity. The poet uses his own person as a symbol of
the present confronting the past, with reverence always but
with no abdication of personality. So Myrrha and Gianni
Schicchi are seen as two of a kind, Pier da Medicina introduces
Curio with a kind of ferocious camaraderie, and Sinon and
Maestro Adamo belabor each other with intimate invective,
caricaturing at the same time that they stress the syncretistic
intent of the poem. No wonder Dante listens with rapt attention! Only in the *Inferno* is such magnificent cosmopolitanism
possible.

Among the nonclassical figures resident in Hell the prepon-
derance is Italian. I count sixty-four Italians as against sixteen
others in this general category (excluding the four biblical figures). Perhaps here it should be noted that in the large, anonymous, vaguely estimated groups, Italians also have a disproportionate representation; it would seem that numerous *Lucchesi*

and Sardinians swim in the pitch of the barrators, and Caccianemico clearly implies that the Bolognese are well represented
among the panders. Florence's name is, as we remember,
"spread through Hell," by now comfortably stocked with
Pisans and Genoese too, if we are to put faith in the poet's
invectives. In any event, of the sixty-four Italians specifically
named the majority (forty-one) are Tuscan, and of these,
twenty-six are Florentines. (Our figures include the otherwise
unidentified "ancient of St. Zita" of Canto XXI, and the anonymous but clearly Florentine suicide of Canto XIII.) Tuscans
also have the widest spread of all Hell's delegations: we find
two of them among the incontinent, three among the heretics,
thirteen with the violent, no less than fourteen included in the
impartially fraudulent (representing five of the ten Malebolge), and a respectable quota of nine authentic traitors. Not
even the classical delegates, all taken together, have such a
wide range, though they come close: of them I find five incontinent, one heretic (we know Epicurus is there although we
do not actually see his tomb), six violent, twelve in the Malebolge (though representing six pouches), and two arch-traitors
(or three, if we assume, as perhaps we should, that Antenor
has come to rest in the ice-zone that bears his name). When
it comes to speaking parts, the Tuscans have twenty-one
out of the entire sixty-five (or sixty-six if Paolo speaks the vindictive line "Caina awaits"; some have thought so and it is
an attractive notion). Of course, as Dante recurrently makes
clear, it is natural that Tuscans should speak more readily than
the rest; after all, their visitor and interlocutor is a compatriot.
On the subject of Tuscans, and in a larger way Italians, it is
interesting to note how many are related: there are three of
the Cavalcanti tribe; two, possibly three, Pazzi; two of either
the Abati or Donati, depending on the identity of Buoso of
Canto XXV; two Ubaldini; and no less than four of the illustrious clan of the Conti Guidi. Some of them have kinsmen in the
other realms too, the house of Swabia and (by now) the
Donati are represented in all three kingdoms. But our pilgrim

will meet only six more fellow-townsmen over the rest of his journey; Hell, the most generous of the realms in its admission policy, is also, in respect to Dante's contacts, the most home-like.

But let us go a little further with our quotas. From the region comprising Emilia, Romagna, and the *Marche*, which had for Dante a kind of social unity, we count twelve representatives, from Lombardy four, from what we might call the Veneto two. From Sardinia also we have two, and one each from Latium, Liguria, and Southern Italy. Cities with more than one representative, aside from Florence, are Bologna with four, and Lucca, Pisa, Pistoia, Padua, and Faenza two each. These figures are, I think, of some interest as signifying what Dante thought of or—more accurately—felt as Italy; they are diversified, but it is notable that some areas are not represented at all, and some very inadequately. Pier and his Emperor must stand for all of Italy south of the Garigliano River, and there are no Venetians to be found in spite of the vivid depiction of their *arsenà* in Canto XXI.

The foreign element requires some distinction in classification. I count among contemporaries or quasi-contemporaries of the poet only four foreigners: one German (if Frederick II may be so counted), two Englishmen, and a Navarrese—the only foreigner with a speaking part. Of course the scope of Infernal demography is not limited to Dante's contemporaries alone; the impression of cosmopolitanism that Hell gives derives from the large contribution made by various traditions of the past. Here the diversity is impressive. Classical figures are numerous; I count some fifty Greeks and twenty-seven Romans. Most of these are mere names in the Limbo catalogs (I include that of *Purgatorio* XXII as well as *Inferno* IV), which include thirty-three Greeks—thirty-four if we count Manto —and twenty-two Romans; it still leaves a substantial number to season Hell's population. Other figures from antiquity not strictly Graeco-Roman but adding their touch of the exotic are Semiramis, Dido, Cleopatra, and the Etruscan Aruns.

Caiaphas, Annas, Potiphar's wife, and of course Judas are from Scripture; from the early Christian centuries we have Pope Anastasius (there, alas, by mistake) and Attila; the Romance tradition gives us four (one lover, two traitors, and the troubadour Bertran de Born), and I count five Arabs. The classical figures have only five "speaking parts" but they have no grounds for complaint since one of them is the eloquent Ulysses, and Virgil is a constant and articulate representative of antiquity. The other categories have only three speaking parts.

The sex census is not without interest. Hell is pretty solidly a man's world; of all the characters even so much as mentioned, only twenty-four are women and, of these, fifteen are Limbo dwellers and so merely names. Of the remaining nine, it is interesting to note that all but one (Manto) have some erotic significance: they include one prostitute and seven illicit lovers. The nature of the sins of Myrrha and Potiphar's wife puts them among the falsifiers for purposes of Dante's categories, but their motivation is lust. There are no women in all the circles of the violent, none in Cocytus; they seem also to have been innocent of gluttony, avarice, and seven out of ten of the lesser kinds of fraud. Even in general categories Dante speaks of them only twice; there are *femmine* in the Limbo and sorry witches among the soothsayers. (Indeed Dante is probably showing his medievalism in this area.) In the *Inferno*, we may add, the only female resident with a speaking part is Francesca (for Beatrice is a transient and Thaïs is merely quoted). There are no children at all (there is nothing, happily, to make us think that Ugolino's sons are Hell dwellers) save for the anonymous *infanti* of Limbo, more tenderly referred to by Virgil as "innocent little ones" in the *Purgatorio*, balancing, as Dante's love for symmetry would require, the "childish voices" of the lower tiers of the celestial rose.

Finally, our census shows that Dante has been faithful to the prescription laid down by Cacciaguida, and in his Hell he has eyes only for the "best people." Even many of the anonymous hordes are made up of souls of distinction, "ladies and knights of old," "popes and cardinals," "scholars of great fame," and the like and, as for the citizens mentioned by name, I can find only one, Asdente, who might claim unconditionally to represent the proletariat. To be sure Vanni Fucci and Ciampolo are both bastards but the former's father was of the Pistoiese Lazzari and, according to Benvenuto, Ciampolo's mother was a noblewoman.

We must not omit, in our summary census of the lower world, the very special and flamboyant sector made up of the monsters, guardians, and officiating demons. These are numerous; "more than a thousand" of Heaven's outcasts line the walls of Dis, an unspecified number of demons lash the panders and seducers, and it seems safe to assume that not all of the *Malebranche* are introduced by name nor, of course, all of the Centaurs. Those specifically identified by my count run to thirty-four. Here too Dante's mixture of breeds and races is noteworthy; the classic tradition supplies the backbone of the corps, from Charon through to five of the six giants ringing the well of Cocytus, but Nimrod and Satan himself may claim a different origin, and Malacoda and his merry men might almost be called contemporary or at least medieval figures. Nor is the fair sex unrepresented in this important caste: the Furies are mentioned by name, and we may suppose that Medusa either actually appears or hovers just behind the wall as Virgil puts his protective hand over Dante's eyes; the Harpies, too, are feminine, as are the keen and savage bitches of the same wood. (Hell does not lack for its fauna.) A surprising number of monsters have speaking parts; all of the vivacious *Malebranche* get in their word, the Furies speak in unison, and seven other "officials" raise their voices in complaint or admonition—indeed two of them, Plutus and Nimrod, have the distinction of having languages of their own.

I do not know whether it has been remarked that Dante gives, demographically at least, to his somber province of eternity (or more correctly, St. Thomas would remind us, aevi-

ternity) a dimension also in time. For Hell's community, as
the traveller Dante knows it, has a past as well as a future.
Those who have been in Hell and have moved on are numerous: all the patriarchs (the catalog of their names in the beginning of Canto IV balances that of the classical spirits mentioned
at the end) and Cato and Trajan and Ripheus—as we learn
from subsequent *cantiche*. There are those yet to come: Boniface, Clement, and of course Gianciotto; the usurers Vitaliano
and Buiamonte; Carlino de' Pazzi; and, as we learn elsewhere,
Forese Donati. (Six Italians, of whom we may note three are
Florentines, to round out the census.) This gives to the season
in Hell a kind of stereoscopic sharpness that is missing alike
from Heaven, which is truly eternal, and from Purgatory,
where all dwellers are transients. Incidentally, there are transients in Hell too, not only Dante Alighieri but Beatrice, who
descends to speak with Virgil in Limbo, and the intervening
angel who opens the gate of Dis.

Much of the fascination of the subterranean journey springs
from Dante's adroit manipulation of the constants in his pattern. Here his formula of repetition with variation is well exemplified. To linger a little over one example: many critics
have noticed the similarities of the stories of Francesca and
Ugolino; in both cases we see a pair, eternally linked by passion, of which one weeps "and weeping speaks" and the other
remains silent. But they do not stand alone; very similar is the
pairing of Ulysses and Diomed, and other duos come readily
to mind—Catalano and Loderingo, Sinon and Maestro
Adamo, the two infuriated Alberti of Cocytus—each pair
subtly distinguished by distribution of lines, attitudes, or char-
acterizations. And there are other groupings too: there are
many rugged individualists like Ciacco or Capaneus or Pier
della Vigna or Brunetto; there are recurrent trios—the three
Florentine sodomites, the three usurers (in both cases alluding
to missing partners), the climactic trinity of treason in Satan's
jaws. Larger groups are exemplified by the thieves, falsifiers,
and traitors, in which the interplay of conversation is general

(I distinguish between such articulate groups and the classical figures of Limbo or the blood-submerged murderers, for the latter are really only catalogs); the liveliest group scene of all is, of course, the *Malebranche* at play.

With infinite art and discretion Dante shifts his focus within the vast range at his disposal; we may note, since we have been speaking of the *Malebranche*, how this spirited portrayal of group action contrasts with the passive and mute parade of the *bolgia* that precedes it and the recurrent pair pattern of the canto immediately following. And as there are shifts of *personae* groupings, so there are shifts of tone and one may say of genre. The high tragedy of Canto v is succeeded by the sordid brutishness of Ciacco, and that in turn by the impersonal contempt of Canto vii, which needs the figure of Fortune to give it any touch of warmth. Again, and more subtly, we may note how the vertiginous and unwholesome metamorphosis of thief into serpent is succeeded by the solemn procession of the false counselors, self-contained in their fiery agony and still preserving their personalities and intellectual superiority—followed in their turn by the mangled yet still defiant figures of the schismatics.

Curtius[9] comments on the cabalistic significance of the numbers in the various groups: there is a "decad" of the violent-against-neighbor category, a "heptad" of sodomites, and the number of illicit lovers specifically named adds up to the "highly symbolic" number nine. (He might have added that it is composed of three classical figures, three Orientals, and three Christians.) But a consideration of Dante's *philarithmia* would take us out of the area of the concrete; for our purposes, it is more to the point to note the variation of plastic groups, skillfully mixed with diversification of genres and even thematic substance. Let us look, for example, at the successive circles of the violent. The murderers and robbers are merely a mute catalog, the conversational charge in this canto (and there is no canto in the whole *Inferno* without conversation) is given the centaurs; no murderer speaks. This is fol-

lowed immediately by the dramatic monologue of Pier della
Vigna, and that circle closes on a note of vigorous action. Another monologue, that of Capaneus, follows, but it is aggressive, where Pier's had been apologetic or defensive; hard upon
it comes Brunetto, the content of whose discourse brings us
from the walls of Thebes back to the familiar Florentine
motif, carried on in the next canto but now by a restless and
agitated trio. A final threesome reinforces the theme of Florence the greedy; again one speaks, while two listen, and a
fourth is mentioned.

We may use the same zone to illustrate how landscape is
utilized to give each setting its particular character: the large
numbers of murderers are bathed in blood, the uneasy throng
of the lowest division prowls, sits, or lies on burning sand; two
individual speakers raise their voices against the same background while another speaks from a contorted tree; one trio
squats in suffering while another plays hide and seek in unholy
shrubbery; landscape, kinetics, and plastic arrangements are
incessantly varied. The whole scope of the *Inferno* would of
course provide many more examples. The symbolism of the
settings has been studied by all commentators and if we were
to consider the reactions of Dante the pilgrim to the various
zones and their inhabitants, we should add another element of
diversification.

No other *cantica* has this kaleidoscopic richness of scene,
action, and personalities, which combine to give its realism a
fascinating diversity and its story line a compelling magnetism.
It would be impossible to read the *Purgatorio* and ignore allegory; it is, as Eliot has said, impossible to read the *Paradiso*
without at least some interest in the doctrine expounded.
There is allegory as well as doctrine in the *Inferno*, but the
reader can forget both as he follows the magnificent narrative
—even though his be a *piccioletta barca*. The articulate and
vigorous inhabitants of the dark world of sin have seen to that
—and the setting against which they display their passion and
their pain has its part in their triumph.

5
The Women of the *Comedy*

ॐ

Let me begin by defining the terms of my subject. In what I shall have to say here, I am ruling out the woman-ideal who, in the person of Beatrice, may be Revelation or a symbol of personal salvation, and similarly Matelda, clearly thought of in much the same level of allegory; and by the same token I exclude such obvious extra-terrestrial characters as Santa Lucia and the Virgin Mary. I mean women considered by the poet without the veil of philosophical-religious allegory, women, as it were, *qua* women. If we except the allegorical figures, so shrouded in the robes of esoteric significance as to be scarcely recognizable as women under their vestments, we shall have, I think, a rather interesting field for exploration and may emerge with some conclusions, possibly not original—what is or could be at this late date in Dante scholarship?—but not without interest as disclosing a side of the poet commonly not put to the fore in this connection.

For in fact, as concerns his views of the other sex, Dante is ambivalent. This may well be his own ambivalence, but it is certainly perfectly in accord with the medieval tradition in which our poet worked. Normally the eyes of the sensitive reader, still in the twentieth century under the influence of the Romantics, focuses on Beatrice and the poet's near worship of her, an attitude not always easy to define in purely personal terms, a relationship in which the sentimental element is as tenuous as it is tender. And here Dante is accepting, passing on, and refining a basic human attitude, undeniably authentic, but cultivated by his predecessors in lyric poetry in a knowing and self-conscious way. Of the thousands of quotations that could be brought in from the Provençal literature, I shall adduce one alone from the very fountainhead of the poets of the *langue d'oc,* William of Poitou, who speaks of his lady as follows:

> Never did mind of man create
> Nor lover's ardent fancy feign
> Such strength of love as binds us twain,
> And one who would our joys relate
> And our delights enumerate
> Would labor half a year in vain.
>
> In her is all nobility
> And worth and valor, birth and fame
> And worldly joys themselves proclaim
> Liege vassals of her sovereignty;
> A man might strive a century
> Nor fairly favor of her claim.
>
> Let her but smile, the sick arise
> And madmen have their wits restored;
> Her frown is a death-dealing sword;
> A glance from her envirtued eyes
> May cast a king down from the skies
> Or from a churl create a lord.[1]

Here, at least in articulate terms, it all began. Later troubadours developed William's conception of the refining and rather terrifying lady goddess; the early Italian poets added intellectual graces to her armament; Guinizelli put her on a par with the angels; and Dante refined her completely, even though he had to kill off the flesh-and-blood creature to allow the supernatural potency to prevail. But for woman, so idealized, death was not a necessary requirement, nor even complete divorce from the flesh. Here and there a Provençal poet will hint at desire, and indeed in the original stages desire was one element in the lady worship, even though it was tacitly assumed, for the most part at least, that passion should lack fulfillment. But from William of Poitou down to Dante the emphasis is on the ennobling qualities of one particular lady whom the poet elects to celebrate and in whom he finds all kinds of exceptional virtues. The stress is on the word exceptional. For this is *one* lady, mysteriously gifted beyond her peers and uniquely shaped for the poet's ennoblement and eventually, in Dantesque terms, salvation. Toward women in general another attitude was in evidence through all the medieval period. In distinction to what I might call the poetic-inspirational, this one might be defined as the clerical-realistic. It has a very long and ancient tradition going back to the Church fathers and the Pauline uneasiness vis-à-vis sex, and, in some segments of society, it is still with us. It is at the furthest remove from idealization, unless it be indeed a kind of negative idealization of its own. It looks symbolically to the wickedness of Eve rather than to the redemptive power of Mary. A few outspoken and eminent authorities may here be cited.

St. Thomas, somewhat hesitantly conceding that woman has a necessary function in the order of nature, nevertheless considered her the result of defective procreation, since "the active power in the male seed tends to the production of a perfect likeness according to the masculine sex." [2] Earlier Church authorities, such as Jerome and Tertullian had had harsher things to say. Even within the lyric tradition, misogyny shows its traces; the second part of the lovers' bible of Andrew the Chaplain is a long catalog of the shortcomings of womankind, and Petrarch too, when not obsessed by Laura, can be quite devastating. In his *De remediis,* speaking in the role of Reason, he congratulates a young man who has had his betrothal broken off, saying that as a man who has lost a wife might be compared to one who had recovered from an illness, one who has lost a fiancée should consider himself as assured of good health.³ No doubt many a simple male, before and after the age of courtly love, shared the impatient view expressed by Leon Battista Alberti: "Women—they are all crazy and full of fleas." ⁴

Now if this tradition is less apparent than the poetic derivation from the love idealization of the Provençal, it is nevertheless present in the works of our poet. I will say nothing of the rather odd passage in the *De vulgari* in which he concludes, for lack of other evidence, that Adam must have spoken first rather than Eve for the simple reason that, representing the nobler of the two sexes, it would be more fitting that he should be the first to use language as an expression of his thought. This is mild enough yet significant; but in the *Comedy*, which I am most concerned with here, there are other indications of his concept of woman, when not wearing a halo. In *Purgatorio* xxix he reproves Eve's presumption, marveling that, where earth and sky obeyed, a mere woman would not suffer any constraint, and adding, somewhat inaccurately, that if she had been properly docile he might have savored the joys of the Earthly Paradise earlier and for a longer time.

Here the phrase "mere woman" (*femmina sola*) obviously carries with it a depreciatory tone. The impudence of the creature, not merely newly formed but a woman! To think that such a low form of life should have excluded us from Paradise! This is the very opposite of the "world well lost for love" concept; it is of course basic to primitive and medieval Christianity. But the most revealing passage of this anti-feministic position occurs somewhat earlier in the *Purgatorio*. In Canto viii, in the vale of the princes, Dante meets Nino Visconti. As many of the souls in Purgatory do, so too does Nino mention those near and dear that he has left behind him. In this case he speaks with bitterness of his wife's remarriage and adds thereto a gratuitous comment on the notorious want of constancy in the weaker sex. Asking Dante to remind his daughter of her father's need for intercession, he says:

> *quando sarai di là da le larghe onde,*
>   *dì a Giovanna mia che per me chiami*
>   *là dove a li 'nnocenti si risponde.*
> *Non credo che la sua madre più m'ami,*
>   *poscia che trasmutò le bianche bende*
>   *le quai convien che, misera, ancor brami.*
> *Per lei assai di lieve si comprende*
>   *quanto in femmina foco d'amor dura,*
>   *se l'occhio o 'l tatto spesso non l'accende.*
>
> (VIII, 70–78)

> (When you have crossed the waters wide once more
> Bid my Giovanna make appeal for me
> Where prayers of innocence obtain response.
> Her mother, I believe, no longer loves me
> Since her white wimples she has put aside,
> Which, hapless woman, she is doomed to rue.
> By her most easily we understand
> How brief the flame of love in woman's heart,
> If not relighted oft by glance or touch.)

It is true of course that Dante himself does not say these lines. But they come after all from the lips of a soul, not in Hell but in Purgatory, and well on its way to salvation. Further, Dante's following terzina seems to add a seal of approval:

> *Così dicea, segnato de la stampa,*
>   *nel suo aspetto, di quel dritto zelo*
>   *che misuratamente in core avvampa.*

> (So spoke he, while on his aspect he bore
> The stamp of that good zeal of righteousness
> That in due measure glows in every breast.)

This is still relatively gentle, but it is certainly along the line of the clerical realists. At her best, according to that theory, woman is an animal, moved only by immediate stimuli and incapable by nature of the firm resolution of her mate. And, further, both quotes carry implicitly in their wording the suggestion that woman is important only in her relation to man. Eve tempted Adam and he fell. Nino's wife could not be faithful to his memory so turned to another man. This is the only noteworthy, if perverse, thing about them.

Now if we turn to the characters of the women that Dante sets before us in the *Comedy*, we shall find this underlying thesis quite effectively developed. How many female characters are there in the *Inferno*, specifically named and identified? The total is 16, of whom 8 appear in Canto IV, 5 in Canto V, and 3 elsewhere. Those in Canto IV are purely literary, put in as a tribute to Virgil or classical literature, and the same may surely be said of Manto, whom we meet among the soothsayers, and, to a lesser degree, of Thaïs, found among the flatterers, and Myrrha, one of the examples of falsifiers of persons. In fact, the only woman from what might be called Dante's own world to appear is Francesca, who is also the only woman with a speaking part. This against a considerable number of well defined and sharply drawn men, ranging from the valiant Farinata to the contemptible Vanni Fucci. At first sight this might look like some evidence either of the superior moral level of women, which we of the twentieth century cheerfully accept, or of Dante's chivalrous nature. In fact I am afraid it signifies simply that Dante thought of woman only in one way: within the love relationship, honorable or otherwise. Indeed, putting aside the ladies of the Limbo as a rather special group, it is interesting to see how he deals with Dido and Cleopatra and Semiramis. Since, as we learn from the incident of Vanni Fucci, the law of Hell requires that the soul tarnished with more than one sin must drop to the circle proper to the graver offense, we should expect to find Dido in the circle of Pier della Vigna and the two other ladies in the river of boiling blood wherein the violently disposed are destined to spend eternity. But Dante saw the three Oriental queens as lustful creatures first and foremost because it was in the love relationship, and that alone, that he thought of women. To look at it another way: in all the circles of Hell, which take in every kind of human infamy, we find the souls of women only in the circles of lust, flattery, and soothsaying—proper womenly avocations according to the clerical-realistic school. It is odd, parenthetically, that the poet did not sharpen his allusion to the witches seen in the twentieth circle by the depiction of some particular female gifted in the art. But in any case, as we discovered in our tour of the Infernal regions, there are no women gluttons in Dante's catalog, none given over to avarice, none in the various levels of violence, none guilty of theft, hypocrisy (surely an odd omission), or treason. As for the falsifier, the unhappy Myrrha, again her sin is caused by perverse love. The absence of female characters in the gallery of simonists and barrators, among others, only goes to show of course that the thirteenth and fourteenth centuries were still a man's world; the absence of certain other classifications (after all, Lady Macbeth was a medieval character) seems to me to indicate that Dante's mind worked as a man's mind would in a man's world. In all the rich gallery of characters of the whole *Inferno*, the only woman that the poet lingers on is Francesca, the woman of love. We shall return to her later.

In the *Purgatorio*, the situation is not quite the same and generalizations are difficult. The number of female characters met with *in toto* is somewhat smaller than that of the *Inferno* (always excluding the purely allegorical, such as Beatrice and Matelda), but among the unforgettable figures in this higher level gallery are two women: Sapia and Pia de' Tolomei. It has always seemed strange to me that Dante did not match his circle of lust in the *Inferno* and his sphere of Venus in the *Paradiso* (both of which contain very articulate ladies) with a female character on the last terrace of the holy mountain. But, no doubt for the best reasons, he doesn't, and so we are left to consider only the aforementioned pair. Since I shall not come back to them again I should like to linger a little on Dante's artistry here. At this point I am not concerned with proving any particular thesis but merely asking the reader to enjoy with me the mastery with which our poet has delineated these characters. Let us recall the episode of Sapia, remarkable, I have always thought, for certain realistic subtleties. Dante, confronting the souls of the envious, whose eyelids are sewn together that they may not see, is moved to compassion but not so great as to prevent him from trying to find out, as he always does, if any of the souls before him be Latin or, as we would say, of Italian stock. And Sapia replies:

> *O frate mio, ciascuna è cittadina*
> *d'una vera città; ma tu vuo' dire*
> *che vivesse in Italia peregrina.*
>
> (XIII, 94–96)

> (O brother, all of us are citizens
> Of a true city: what you mean is one
> Who as a pilgrim dwelt in Italy.)

She then goes on to speak with a certain complacency, it seems to me, of the enormity of her sinful nature, her ultimate repentance, and the intervention of the holy Pier, which had shortened her sojourn on the outer shore of the mount. When, pausing at last to inquire of Dante's identity, she learns that he is still in the flesh, she asks him to remember her in his prayers and adds, a little gratuitously:

> *E cheggioti, per quel tu più brami*
> *se mai calchi la terra di Toscana,*
> *che a' miei propinqui tu ben mi rinfami*
> *Tu li vedrai tra quella gente vana*
> *che spera in Talamone, e perderagli*
> *più di speranza ch'a trovar la Diana;*
> *Ma più vi perderanno li ammiragli.*
>
> (XIII, 148–154)

> (And I beseech you, by your heart's desire,
> If ever you put foot on Tuscan soil,

> Give me good name again among my kin;
> You'll find them 'mongst that empty-headed folk
> Who trust in Talamone but therein
> Will lose more hope than e'er Diana cost—
> Aye, and the admirals will lose the most.)

What gives this character flesh and blood is the tension of contradictory elements. She is after all a saved soul, and presumably her better nature has triumphed; we must not question the sincerity of her gratitude to Pier Pettinaio. At the same time in the way she picks Dante up, setting his theology straight among other things, and particularly in the contempt she still maintains for her old neighbors, there is clear portrayal of a certain type of female with which we are all familiar—self-assured, a little bossy, somewhat waspish. I should add perhaps that not all commentators hear in her initial correction of Dante the same tone that I do: *"come suona nuova fresca e delicata la voce di quest' anima,"* says Momigliano. But this is an unusual reaction. Provenzal, among others, feels as I do—and with a rather original tangent of his own; as one who, for envy of her neighbors, had never loved her native town, says he, Sapia is glad to point out to Dante that earthly attachments to city or region are inappropriate to the Christian. And Sapegno remarks on her "bitter and pungent detachment" from the affairs of Siena as evidenced in her remarks about the vanity and folly of the Sienese. But I find *quella gente vana* (that empty-headed folk) a phrase more indicative of censure than detachment. The remains of envy are still there, and, as most of the characters in Purgatory, Sapia is, to me at least, still earth-bound.

I have reversed the Dantesque order in my discussion of the two female representatives in Purgatory because I prefer to linger on Pia the gentle rather than on Sapia the still acidulous. And surely the evocation of Pia is one of the masterpieces of Dante. We are in Canto v, still in the ante-Purgatory, among the souls whose penance was delayed until their death by violence. This is how we know what happened to Pia, for she does not herself linger on the details of her own story. Bonconte da Montefeltro has just finished his long, rather melodramatic, account of his death and the subsequent disposition of his earthly remains and, as one who has listened patiently, nor is desirous of inflicting her own suffering on others but in simple obedience to the law of Purgatory whereby souls look to the prayers of the faithful on earth to help them, Pia speaks out. In Dante's words:

> "*Deh, quando tu sarai tornato al mondo,*
> *e riposato de la lunga via*"
> seguitò il terzo spirito al secondo,
> "*ricorditi di me che son la Pia:*
> *Siena mi fè; disfecemi Maremma:*
> *salsi colui che 'nnanellata pria*
> *disposando m'avea con la sua gemma.*"
>
> (v, 130–136)

> (Then a third
> Spoke, saying: "When you are once more returned
> Into the world and after your long road
> Have taken your repose, remember me;
> Pia am I; Siena gave me life,
> Maremma death, as he well knows who first
> Betrothed me, then espoused me with his ring.")

In seven brief lines what a beautiful picture is painted! Pia tells her name as she must, but does not linger on her family, which was noble and prominent. Most modern commentators, following the *Anonimo fiorentino* and Benvenuto, identify her as Pia de' Tolomei of Siena, married to Nello de' Pannocchieschi, lord of the castle of Pietra, not far from Massa Marittima. She carefully avoids any personal accusation; she does not say that she died at the hands of her husband, only *Maremma mi disfece*, as if to imply that her destiny was a matter of geography. But yet she is a woman, and womanly reproach as well as melancholy is certainly apparent in the lines recalling that the very one who had married her and pledged his faith with his ring is the one tragically familiar with the details of her death. But, most of all, the commentators, with reason, have fastened on her opening lines as truly revealing of gentleness and courtesy in the highest sense of the words. Provenzal speaks of her *femminile gentilezza;* Hatzfeld in his *Lettura dantesca* for this canto, remarks: *È veramente una preghiera femminile, dolce, piena di delicatezza e di carità.*" [5] (It is indeed a womanly prayer, sweet and full of delicacy and charity.) She, like the other souls, is eager for Dante's prayers, and perhaps she has greater need than others since it is unlikely she will get them from her husband. And so she makes her request. But only with a consideration and a solicitude for Dante, truly unique. She is the only individual whom Dante meets among the souls of the mountainside who really thinks of Dante's condition. "After you have had a rest, if you have the time I hope you will think of me." A real lady, as rare in the *Comedy* as they are in life.

A good deal of the charm of Pia springs from her reticence: Francesca had been reticent too, we remember, and Dante had been obliged to coax her for further particulars of her case. But Pia is even more reserved. As with many of Dante's brief sketches, so in the case of Pia there is lacking real historical evidence which would enable us to fill in the gaps. Two stories are told by various ancient commentators: one that her husband did away with her because he wanted to marry another woman, the second presenting Pia herself as blameworthy, or at least vulnerable to her husband's suspicion of her fidelity. In this case she would be another Francesca perhaps, but to me the wording of her tale suggests the former interpretation. In any case it is again a love relationship which is the central part of her crisis and which attracts the interest of our poet.

Let us, in this cursory survey, take leave now of Purgatory, noting once more the negative aspect of our argument: here are the traditional Christian sins of Pride, Envy, Anger, Sloth,

Avarice, Gluttony, and Lust, and in only one of the terraces do we meet a woman. In the ante-Purgatory of Dante's own invention, the recently arrived, the excommunicate, the tardy penitents, the unprepared—in only one of these categories do we meet a woman. Men have a clear monopoly on Pride, Anger, Sloth, Avarice, Gluttony, and, strangely, as we have noted, even Lust.

In the *Paradiso* we do not find the proportion much altered nor the underlying implications of Dante's exhibits either. In this realm everyone we meet is a saint, and we must assume that the incidence of sanctity is much the same in either sex. I think this may be implied in the seating arrangements of the true heaven, where a row of Old Testament women faces a row of Christian male saints across the heavenly rose. But in fact the souls of women present themselves to Dante the Wayfarer only in two of the ten heavens: in the moon and—naturally, one might say—in Venus. In the moon our pilgrim meets the inconstant; that is to say, those whose wills were right-directed but who were in some way ineffectual in their pursuit of their goals on earth, or, it may be, a little shallow in their capacity for entertaining the vision. To exemplify this group Dante selects two nuns who, on earth, were compelled to break their vows. There must have been quite a few monks who suffered the same unhappy fate, but it is significant that Dante chooses to exemplify this class by nuns. Is there here an implication that inconstancy may be expected from the gentler sex, buttressing the remarks of Nino Visconti in the *Purgatorio*? I am inclined to think there is.

We may, as defenders of the virtues of womanhood, observe with pleasure that Dante has put some of the most beautiful words of the *Paradiso* into the mouth of Piccarda, who has the cue speaking role for this sphere. He also allows her to express a dogma that is the very key to understanding the hierarchy and the psychology of that happy realm. For, on his venturing to ask her if she is satisfied with the lowest sphere of

Paradise, he has from her an answer that not only contents the questioner but must, I think, inspire the reader:

> *Anzi è formale ad esto beato esse*
> *tenersi dentro a la divina voglia,*
> *per ch'una fansi nostre voglie stesse:*
> *sì che, come noi sem di soglia in soglia*
> *per questo regno, a tutto il regno piace*
> *com'a lo re ch'a suo voler ne invoglia.*
> *E'n la sua volontade è nostra pace:*
> *ell'è quel mare al qual tutto si move*
> *ciò ch'ella cria e che natura face.*
>
> (III, 79–82)

> (Nay, rather, 'tis the essence of our state
> To hold ourselves within that will divine
> Through which our own wills are themselves made one.
> Our disposition thus from sill to sill
> Is pleasing to the realm entire no less
> Than to the King Whose wish is our desire.
> In His will is our peace; it is the sea
> To which all things are drawn that it creates
> Or which the work of nature may produce.)

Piccarda then, with a modesty at once appropriate to a great lady and a saint, presents the soul of Constance, mother of Frederick II. We may admire the delicacy with which she passes over the harsh vicissitudes of her own life, while yet telling our poet what he has a right to know about her, and moves gracefully on to focus Dante's attention on another.

> "Perfetta vita e alto merto inciela
> donna più su" mi disse "a la cui norma
> nel vostro mondo giù si veste e vela,
> perchè fino al morir si vegghi e dorma
> con quello sposo ch'ogni voto accetta
> che caritate a suo piacer conforma.

Dal mondo, per seguirla, giovinetta
fuggi'mi, e nel suo abito mi chiusi,
e promisi la via de la sua setta.
Uomini poi, a mal più ch'a bene usi,
fuor mi rapiron de la dolce chiostra:
Iddio si sa qual poi mia vita fusi.
E quest'altro splendor che ti si mostra
de la mia destra parte e che s'accende
di tutto il lume de la spera nostra,
ciò ch'io dico di me, di sé intende:
sorella fu, e così le fu tolta
di capo l'ombra de lo sacre bende.
Ma poi che pur al mondo fu rivolta
contra suo grado e contra buona usanza,
non fu dal vel del cor già mai disciolta.
Quest'è la luce della gran Costanza
che del secondo vento di Soave
generò il terzo e l'ultima possanza."

(III, 97–120)

("Perfected life and high desert," she said,
"Enheaven above a lady by whose rule
Habit and veil some put on in your world,
So until death come they may watch and sleep
With that Spouse who accepts all vows which love
Shapes in conformity with his desire.
While yet a girl to follow her I fled
The world and donned her habit, promising
To keep the pathway of her sisterhood.
Thereafter men, more used to ill than good
Tore me from that sweet cloister; only God
Knows what my life became from that day on.
This other splendor who reveals herself
Upon my right and who is luminous
With all the light pertaining to our sphere
Takes to herself all I have said of me;
Like me a nun and likewise from her brow
The shadow of the sacred veil was torn.
But though brought back into the world again

> Against her will, against all decency,
> She never was despoiled of the heart's veil.
> This is the light of the great Constance, she
> Who from the second blast of Swabia
> Conceived the third and final puissance.")

Constance herself does not speak, and Piccarda, her task done, an *Ave Maria* on her lips, disappears, *come per acqua cupa cosa grave*, (as weighty objects sink beneath the waves) surely one of the most musical lines in the *Comedy*. . . . A-propos of these ladies whose fate on earth was so similar, we may note that they have a similar relationship in one of Dante's minor devices for linking his realms together and for the exemplification of dogma. For the Donati and the Swabian royal family are uniquely endowed with representatives in all the realms of Dante's other world. Piccarda's brother Forese is met by Dante in Purgatory and from Forese Dante learns that another brother, the Black chieftain Corso, is destined to ultimate residence in Hell. Likewise we have met Manfred, Constance's grandson, wandering in the ante-Purgatory—who could forget the line *biondo e bello e di gentile aspetto* (of gentle mien and blond and fair)?—while the great Emperor himself somewhat alleviates by his illustrious company the sufferings of Farinata. Of both trios it is only the woman who attains salvation.

A much more vigorous and enigmatic character awaits us in the Heaven of Venus. This is, to be sure, a sphere rich in lofty and eloquent spirits: an entire canto is dedicated to the discourse of Prince Charles Martel, whom Dante had known as a young man, and, in the successive Canto ix, we meet the souls of Cunizza da Romano, Folquet de Marseille, and Rahab, two women and one man. Rahab does not speak and Folquet is not to our purpose here, but concerning Cunizza there is much to be said. First let us see what she has to say for herself:

> *In quella parte de la terra prava*
> *italica che siede tra Rialto*

> *e le fontane di Brenta e di Piava,*
> *si leva un colle, e non surge molt'alto,*
> *là onde scese già una facella*
> *che fece a la contrada un grande assalto.*
> *D'una radice nacqui e io ed ella:*
> *Cunizza fui chiamata, e qui refulgo*
> *perché mi vinse il lume d'esta stella.*
> *Ma lietamente a me medesma indulgo*
> *la cagion di mia sorte, e non mi noia;*
> *che parria forse forte al vostro vulgo.*
>
> (IX, 25–36)

> (In Italy, wicked land, within the march
> That lies between Rialto and the source
> Of Brenta and Piave stands a hill,
> Rising not over high, from whence long since
> A torch came down to waste the countryside;
> Of that same torch's root I sprang; Cunizza
> I was called and here I scintillate
> Because this planet's light held me enthralled.
> Yet joyfully within me I approve
> The occasion of my lot, nor am displeased;
> Which might seem strange to your unlettered herd.)

Then follow twenty-eight more lines, six dedicated to praise of Folquet de Marseille and the rest to a survey of dire events destined to befall the inhabitants of northeast Italy.

Not only the *vulgo* but such scholars as Scartazzini ("*Perché Dante la mettesse in Paradiso è difficile indovinare*") have been puzzled at finding this jaunty lady in such high company. To be sure, she serves some of Dante's purposes very well. Like Piccarda and Constance, she is—for the perceptive student of the *Comedy*—a link with other incidents and themes in the poem. For, as we read her autobiographical sketch, we are reminded by her own words of her brother Ezzelino, faithful henchman of the Emperor and by many of his enemies thought to have been begotten of the devil.

And we are reminded, as in the case of Piccarda, of the inscrutable workings of Providence through nature as laid down by Charles Martel in the preceding canto: he had cited us the example of Jacob and Esau, thus laying the ground for a contemporary illustration of the same principle. Nor is this all: a reader of Dante's own time would not hear the name Cunizza without thinking at once of Sordello, since one of the more scandalous episodes in the life of this lady was her abduction by the troubadour of Goito. And recalling Sordello, the reader's mind plays over the Provençal thread: we think of Arnaut Daniel and Bertran de Born, and we feel the aura of love, lawlessness, and poetry that hovers around such characters, and so are the better prepared, whether or not we are consciously aware of it, for the appearance of yet another troubadour, who, through this perilous maze of lust and valor, has found his way to salvation. Cunizza's connections may be yet further traced: she is related to the Alberti of Mangone, two of whose members we have seen locked fast in the ice of Cocytus. And her reference to the untimely end of Riccardo da Cammino makes us think too of the good Gherardo of *Purgatorio* xvi—and thus another cord of association is made fast. She is also of course a convenient and appropriate mouthpiece for Dante's enumeration of the misdeeds of his political enemies: Bianchi thought she was chosen, being the sister of a ferocious Ghibelline, because most apt to predict the woes of the Guelphs. But the principal reason she is here is to illustrate a point of dogma. The ways of God are mysterious and the strangest path may lead to salvation. And once this is achieved, what can we do but look back with satisfaction on our journey? St. Augustine says something of that nature in his *Confessions*. Here is a woman who has sinned frequently and, so far as we can tell from the records, joyously. Not once but many times. I will not excite the reader's imagination by recounting the details, but they are lively and well documented. To be sure, Edmund Gardner, with the chivalry of a late

Victorian gentleman, thinks that Cunizza may have been as much sinned against as sinning,[6] but Benvenuto da Imola, who was several centuries closer to the records, does not hesitate to describe her as "a child of Venus." And freely here before us she admits that the star in which she now dwells had too much influence on her in her youth. Happily for her, she did not die in youth but lived to the age where one "furls the sails and clues the sheets," as another of Dante's elderly penitents had put it. God gave her time and she used it to good advantage. So, since the path she had followed eventually led her to salvation, how could she have any regrets? Nay, she looks back on those tumultuous years with a sense of satisfaction bordering on complacency. What a contrast to the tender Francesca, who, in Dante's version at least, had sinned but once, and that once out of love, not wantonness, and yet, having had no time given her, having come unprepared to her last hour, flutters now in Hell on the eternal whirlwind, her only satisfaction being the vindictive assurance that her slayer will eventually find his place even lower than hers.

Now the contrast between the destinies of Francesca and Cunizza serves to reinforce another central point of Christian dogma: to wit that one's eternal condition depends upon the state of the soul at the moment of death. But there may be more to it than that; perhaps we can see some justification for Dante's disposition even in human terms. So I should like to go back now to Francesca's story. No reader of Dante need be reminded of the seductive appeal of her words, beginning with the address to Dante, almost as considerate as Pia's lines quoted above:

> *O animal grazioso e benigno*
>   *che visitando vai per l'aere perso*
>   *noi che tignemmo il mondo di sanguigno,*
> *se fosse amico il re de l'universo,*
>   *noi pregheremmo lui de la tua pace,*
>   *poi c'hai pietà del nostro mal perverso.*
>
> (v, 88–93)

> (O living soul, compassionate and kind,
> Coming through the dark air to look on us,
> Who left a stain of crimson in the world,
> If the great Lord of all were but our friend
> We should make prayer to him for your peace
> Since you have pity for our perverse ill.)

and concluding with the famous line of delicate reticence:

> *quel giorno più non vi leggemmo avante.*

> (That day we read no more therein.)

This is, as everyone knows, one of the most moving episodes in the *Comedy*. And, emotionally if not dogmatically, Dante is on Francesca's side. (At least the wayfarer is: clearly the poet himself, whatever be his feelings, knows where she belongs.) So are the overwhelming majority of commentators. Scartazzini, to be sure, remarked that, while esthetic beauty could be found in the Francesca episode, moral beauty was totally lacking, but De Sanctis speaks for the great majority of readers when he says:

"Francesca is a woman and nothing but a woman, she is a complete poetic personality of Homeric clarity. True, she is ideal, but she is not the ideal of something else; she is the ideal of herself, and an ideal perfectly realized, with a wealth of attributes that give her all the semblance of a living person. Her traits—love, gentility, purity, modesty, charm—are already found in all the concepts of woman prevalent in the poetry of the time; but in her case these traits are not mere epithets, but the true qualities of a real person, qualities that are operative and therefore alive." [7]

But is Francesca all this sweet? Recently Dorothy Sayers has come forth with a sharper distinction. Perhaps it takes a woman to know a woman. Anyway, this is what she has to say, seeing in Francesca what she calls the egotism of the damned:

"Even at his tenderest, Dante deals ruthlessly with this egotism; listen to Francesca: 'If the King of the Universe were our friend'—one begins to think it is all God's fault; 'Love took hold of us'—well, Love (as Dante had once said) is an abstraction, an accident in a substance; are we to put the blame on an abstraction? 'My beautiful body was torn from me, I had no time to repent—' and then, like the lash of a whip, the sudden savage snarl: 'Cain's place awaits our murderer!'* The soft voice resumes: 'You are so kind—I will tell you how it was; we were reading that lovely story—we thought no harm —something came over Paolo and he kissed me—the book was a pander and he that wrote it!' God, Love, Gianciotto, the novelist, were to blame, not we; we were the helpless prey of our own and other people's passions, and now we drift on the black wind.

"So piteous are the accents here, and so moving the sheer poetry that it might deceive the very elect. Many indeed have been deceived into swallowing Francesca's version of things, hook, line and sinker, and transferring to Dante the resentment they feel on her behalf against God, love, vindictive husbands, 'suggestive' literature and all the rest of it." [8]

And pondering a little on this line of argument, with every willingness to accept with sympathy the picture of the love-tossed and love-betrayed heroine of the fifth canto, yet there is, compared to Cunizza, a kind of egocentricity if not egotism in her. All her story is about herself and her tragic love: there may be even a kind of narcissism in the phrase *la bella persona che mi fu tolta* (the fair body that was reft from me). Cunizza has a larger scope: she is able to give Dante an account of things to happen in her native region, the affairs of which, it would seem, she still follows with interest. She is able to feel strong indignation for social and political injustices which do

* But is the line really hers? I find the suggestion, originally made by E. Roncaglia and picked up by Donadoni, that it may more correctly be assigned to Paolo, very appealing. But the notion has not met with general favor. (E. Donadoni, "Le tre donne della *Commedia*" in *Studi danteschi e manzoniani*, Florence, 1963, p. 80.)

not affect her personally. (So much so in fact that she may be regarded as still too much involved with terrestrial and parochial affairs to be a fitting citizen of the eternal city.) A kind of altruism she has, a kind of generosity of temperament, which in a way makes her sin almost irrelevant. Perhaps she was not so much a lustful woman as a generous woman; though her sin was as grave as Francesca's and more frequent, yet it was not, to the same degree, self-indulgent. I am inclined to think that in the varying fates of these two ladies Dante was not merely illustrating a point of dogma but drawing a picture of two different kinds of temperament: one, intense, tragic, beautiful if you will, but self-centered; the other kindly, careless it may be of one or two laws of moral behavior, but with an element of genuine unselfishness. Perhaps, had she been killed at the moment of sin as Francesca was, she yet would have found the necessary second in which to repent because after all she had not been totally involved in the sin—perhaps had Francesca lived to repent it would never have occurred to her to do so because of total commitment to her own self-indulgence. Or perhaps the wisdom and the outgoing nature of Cunizza can come only with age and she was merely lucky. There are people, one sees them or senses them, somehow destined to pass through the fire safely, others whose lot is to be consumed by it. Truly, as Dante says himself, who can fathom the divine predestination?

I suppose in conclusion we have found only what we might have expected to find. The range of female characters in the *Comedy* is limited because the range of a woman's activities in Dante's time was limited. And if there were, as there must have been, women who committed sins represented only by male characters in the *Comedy*, they were, by nature of the social milieu, not so prominent as the men and so not such good examples for the instruction of posterity, and prominent examples our poet must have, if he is to follow the advice of old Cacciaguida. We should give thanks rather for the few we do have: Francesca, Sapia, Pia, Piccarda, Cunizza—it is as varied a group as a medieval poet could have given us, and in fact more varied than any other I can think of. No doubt he could do better nowadays—but can a woman's world produce a *Divine Comedy*?

6
Dante's Provençal Gallery

In Chapter Two of the second book of his *De vulgari eloquentia* Dante defines the "capital matters that ought to be treated supremely" by poets. They are three: "safety, love, and virtue," which are spelled out in specific language as "prowess in arms, the fire of love, and the direction of the will." He adds that "the illustrious writers have written poetry in the vulgar tongue on these subjects exclusively, namely Bertran de Born on Arms, Arnaut Daniel on Love, Giraut de Bornelh on Righteousness, Cino of Pistoia on Love, his friend on Righteousness . . . I do not find however that any Italian has as yet written poetry on the subject of arms."[1] The passage well exemplifies Dante's fondness for categories and where possible, symmetry: three subjects, three poets (at least when a gallery is complete, as the Provençal is and the Italian not yet). Knowing Dante's attachment to his authorities and his cult of three, one could almost predict that if he were to write a great poem it would have three divisions and each would contain a representative of the "vulgar" tongue, which had been such an inspiration to him and other writers in their own vernacular. And so, in fact, it comes out: of all Dante's triads the Provençal poets are most obviously and architectonically disposed, one for each *cantica*, each one clearly identified and prominently placed, varying only, I would say, in their degree of integration with their milieu. But before venturing any further statement on the group as a whole, I should like to pass the chosen troubadours in review.

Bertran de Born's dramatic and macabre appearance in the *bolgia* of the sowers of discord (*Inf.* xxviii, 112 ff.) will not easily be forgotten. He appears carrying his own severed head in his hand *a guisa di lanterna* (as a man carries a lantern). Approaching Dante, he raises his arm *con tutta la testa* (with the whole head), a gesture of *naturalezza spaventosa* (frightful naturalness);[2] the movement of the line, as Crescini remarks,[3] underlines the painful effort required. Frightful the scene is, to be sure, although the grotesque here all but verges on the comic. Where Dante got the notion of the portable head, scholars have been unable to find out with any certainty; the roots are probably in folklore and myth and most American readers—of my generation at least—are prepared for the weird spectacle by the stratagem of Brom Van Brunt, in the "Legend of Sleepy Hollow." Washington Irving, as has been pointed out by various critics,[4] owed much to German folklore; probably even before Orpheus' head rolled down the Hebrus pathetically calling on Eurydice as memorialized in the *Georgics*, the sight that terrified Ichabod Crane was familiar to our fanciful ancestors. Joyce's Virag illustrates that the image continues to have an appeal. Cases have been cited from the old literatures, Indian, Gaelic, and Icelandic, to say nothing of Gawain's odd encounter.[5] The Church too includes various *cefalofori* among its saints; St. Denis is perhaps the most famous, but the category includes also San Miniato, surely well known to Dante.

As Bertran—or so he claims—has severed the head, that is, the father of the family, from his son, the punishment is admitted by the sinner himself to have its appropriateness. It is commonly accepted that Bertran's function here is to illustrate one sub-species of the sowers of discord. As Mohammed and Ali had created sectarian schisms and Curio and Mosca dissension in country and city, so Bertran exemplifies the same divisive role within the family, a smaller unit to be sure, but the sin, being more personal, is somehow more malicious. Bertran is the last of the categories cited, as if to suggest a final grade of wickedness. Furthermore, the *discordia domestica* here exemplified had wider repercussions: since Bertran set kings at each other, his machinations had political as well as familial consequences. Bertran, standing for one category, serves also to sum up all of them.

The detached head is properly articulate and indeed even eloquent. Bertran defines his sin with a rather pretentious scriptural reference, giving it a certain dignity of tradition, as it were, and assigning to himself a rôle of importance perhaps out of proportion to historical truth. (Crescini, among others, believes that Bertran somewhat exaggerates his political importance, but Dante took him at his word—or the word of the Provençal biography.)

But if Dante treats the old warrior with a certain respect, it is hardly a matter for surprise. We have noted the reference in the *De vulgari*; in the *Convivio* (IV, ii) Dante had spoken of Bertran's generosity, and if we are to be surprised at all, it is perhaps rather to find such a fine gentleman in such an unpleasant predicament. But of course—as for Farinata, Jason, Ulysses, and others—it is precisely Bertran's stature that makes him an appropriate choice—in keeping with the suggestion laid down by Cacciaguida before Dante sat down to write his story. As for the long vexed question of *re giovane* as against *re Giovanni* in line 135, all modern commentators have agreed on the former reading even though it is supported by only a minority of the manuscripts and, worse, gives the line a very irregular (though not unique) metrical pattern. *Giovane* is preferred simply because critics have been unable to believe that Dante, knowing anything of Bertran at all, could fail to know of his friendship with the "young king" and of the latter's feud with his father. But along these lines something more may be said with respect to the canto we have before us.

In spite of the careful and exhaustive work of many scholars, much of Dante's acquaintance with the troubadours must remain conjectural. Santangelo argues that our poet had not studied them (although he knew about them of course) at the time of the composition of the *Vita nuova*;[6] but when he undertook the *De vulgari eloquentia* (1304–05) he showed at least a superficial expertise in the field. I say at least superficial because his choice of exemplary poems seems sometimes a little capricious. The one he cites to show the virtues of Bertran, for example (*De vulgari eloquentia*, Chapter II), is a rather undistinguished *sirventes* (most anthologies ignore it, but the text may be found in Chaytor's *Troubadours of Dante*) and one cannot but wonder specifically what other poems were known to him. Perhaps Fraticelli is right in finding a clue in this very *re giovane* (young king).[7] For in the celebrated lament for the ill-starred first-born of Henry, the phrase *giove re ingles* (young English king) recurs in every stanza. It is Bertran's finest poem and it is not unlikely that Dante knew it and deliberately echoes the key phrase here. And if he did know it he would know too the first line, *Si tuit li dol e·lh plor e·lh marrimen* or, as Ezra Pound puts it:

> If all the grief and woe and bitterness
> All dolour, ill and every evil chance
> That ever came upon this grieving world
> Were set together they would seem but light
> Against the death of the young English king.[8]

And if he knew those first lines, surely he had them in mind in his own introductory passage in *Inferno* xxviii (lines 7–21), where he says that if all the mangled and mutilated of the many wars in Southern Italy were brought together it would be nothing compared to the sum of horrors that met his eyes in this *bolgia*. Of the modern commentators only Sapegno picks this up;[9] he cites no authority for his observation and I have not found it among any of the older editors I have consulted, though Vossler comes close to saying as much. Yet merely to put the passages side by side seems proof sufficient: in rhythm, grammatical construction, and even their emotional element they match perfectly, although Dante's correlatives are concrete and not abstract.

Perhaps we can go a little further along this line of plausible conjecture. If Dante's bloody picture of the battlefield strewn with mutilated humanity has a literary source, the most probable one is to be found in some of Bertran's other verses. Celebrated, for example, is the famous *Miei sirventes vuolh far de·ls res amdos* (I'll make a half *sirventes* for two kings)— the term itself is suggestive of division as well as contempt— the ghastly imagery of which is very close to that of Dante:

> If both kings are brave and courageous we shall soon see fields strewn with quartered bodies, helmets, swords, shields, and saddles, and warriors cleft from bust to breeches, and we shall see many a horse roam riderless, and many a lance protruding from breast or flank. . . .

In his *sirventes Be·m platz lo gais temps de pascor* (I love the gay springtime), called by Croce a *lieto grido di battaglia* (a happy battle cry),[10] Bertran speaks of seeing, in similar fray, arms dented and pierced, soldiery with no other thought than to "split heads and limbs," and again "the dead with the blood-stained lance tips in their flanks." It is worth noting that this poem too contains the word *acesmatz* (fixed up) which Dante italianizes in line 37 of this canto; here it is the presiding demon who "fixes up" his victims for their blood tour of the circle. Almost all commentators note that Dante's *accisma* is a Provençalism; few remark that it is the only use of the word in the *Comedy*. In fact it is extremely rare in Italian; Battaglia gives only one other example (from the seventeenth-century Menzini—clearly an echo of Dante's line). The derivation of the Provençal word is uncertain (see Körting, Meyer-Lübke, Battaglia, and Hoare for a wide range of choice). The relationship to *scisma* may be phonetic rather than etymological (though Spitzer and Schiaffini postulate an "*adschismare*" [11]),

but Dante surely intended a connection. Whatever the ety-
mology, I think that Dante thought of it as a Provençalism
and that the word is a linguistic token of the presence of Bertran from the very beginning of the canto. His aura carries
over into the next canto as well: Dante, reproached for his
obsession with the gruesome sights before him, can only answer that he was fascinated by the spectacle of the lord of
Altaforte. The place-name here would remind the informed
reader of the siege of Hautefort and the capture of Bertran by
the irate king Henry and so of the story of all the intrigue and
resentment surrounding the troubadour and his royal associates. But Dante's excuse, which is also a confession, is more
significant on another level; he has been infected by Bertran's
bloodlust (as the imagery cited shows), and—*contrapasso*
within *contrapasso*—Bertran who had surveyed so many
corpse-strewn battlefields with something close to delight is
now the object of like contemplation—just another of the
many *mortz e nafratz* and well *acesmatz* to boot.

As a character Bertran is curiously one-dimensional; far
from being ashamed of his sin he thrusts himself on Dante,
apparently eager to make himself known and to have his presence reported (*E perchè tu di me novella porti*), and tells with
apparent complacency of his instigation of hostility between
father and son. He finds a certain satisfaction, we feel, in his
spiritual kinship with Achitophel and perhaps also in his
knowledge of Scripture; he seems in his last line to be trying to
give the impression that the law of *contrapasso* has been designed for him. All the sowers of discord have something of
the same characteristics; Bertran seems perhaps a little more
aggressive in his self-assurance and very much aware of the
effect his grotesque appearance is creating. This is in fact quite
in keeping with the *autoritratto* he gives in his own verses,
which reveal a militant self-confidence and a touch of exhibi-
tionism. He is an isolated figure too; even Mohammed has a
kinsman with him, and the other sinners of the *bolgia* are
linked by blood or regional origin. Bertran stands alone. He is

alone likewise in his associations within the *Comedy*. There is a faint reminiscence of his gesture in Manfred's display of his wounds in *Purgatorio* III, but, in the significant sense in which Farinata prepares us for Sordello or Cacciaguida recalls Brunetto, there is no correspondence for Bertran, somber, grim, and forever isolated.

So far as the rôle of Arnaut (the Purgatorial Provençal) is concerned, it may be said to be the simplest of all of the characters under discussion here. On the terrace of lust he is not so much an actor as an exhibit; presented by the modest Guinizelli as the *miglior fabbro del parlar materno* (best wordsmith of the mother tongue), and the one who in *versi d'amore e prose di romanzi/ soverchiò tutti*, he identifies himself in a courtly opening phrase, in substance very similar to that of Pier della Vigna's, and (with a few words borrowed from Folquet de Marseille) expresses regret for his past follies, his hope for the future, and bids Dante to remember "in time" his suffering. There is no real dialog between him and Dante and, as various commentators have noted, there is an air of detachment about him. (Momigliano is reminded of Pia.) As he steps forth from the fire he unobtrusively rounds out a poetic group almost as large as that in Limbo, where Dante had been *sesto tra cotanto senno* (sixth among such great intellects). Here he is fifth—at least in chronological order. The sequence is suggestive and in itself poetic enough to dwell upon: the classical Virgil, the late Latin Statius, the first of the "new poets" (see the *Vita nuova*), Arnaut, the founder of the *dolce stil nuovo*, and Dante himself. A gallery richer in its variety and considerably more articulate (for each of the five at one point or another has his say) than that of the supreme but rather remote classical figures of *Inferno* IV.

Critics past and present have been fascinated by Dante's Arnaut, more specifically by Dante's concept of him and his place in literature. To touch first on a minor aspect of his case, the argument has raged long and loud over the meaning of the lines quoted above (*Purg.* XXVI, 118–119). A first reading would justify the implication that Arnaut had written not only lyrics (*versi d'amore*), but also prose romances, and it was indeed Tasso who first ascribed to him a version of the Lancelot, which enabled later critics to make much of his association with *Inferno* v. As recently as 1952 Bowra seemed willing to accept his authorship not only of a *Lancelot* but also of a *Rinaldo* attributed to Arnaut by Luigi Pulci. Bowra believed simply that these *prose di romanzi* were lost.[12] Gianluigi Toja however, Arnaut's most recent editor, after an exhaustive examination of the subject, rejects any such hypothesis and concludes by quoting with approval Viscardi's verdict that Dante meant simply that "Arnaut was the greatest of all who had written in the vernacular, in verse or in prose." [13] And indeed with some slight manipulation of the syntax the passage may be fairly translated, "He surpassed all [who wrote either] verses of love or adventure tales in prose," which could be paraphrased, "he was best of all users of their mother tongue, whether they be the Provençal love poets or the French composers of romances in prose."

A much more provocative question is why Dante so greatly admired Arnaut. There is ample evidence, outside of Guinizelli's warm praise in this passage, that he had great esteem for him. He mentions him three times in the *De vulgari*, and he renders him the highest tribute of all—imitation. His sestina is clearly written in rivalry of Arnaut, as is his "double sestina," as the passage in the *De vulgari eloquentia* indicates. All of the *Petrose* show some trace of Danielism whether it be in their *caras rimas*, their violent rhythms, or the tormented emotional atmosphere they suggest. It is not easy to understand Dante's admiration for a poet who seems very often willfully obscure and exhibitionistic, and, in sheer substance, either incomprehensible or platitudinous. Grandgent, I think, spoke for not only his own but all modern generations when, allowing for Arnaut's virtues, he finds him, nevertheless, "one of the most laborious and tiresome of the Provençal versifiers," [14] and even Bowra, anxious to explain Dante's devotion to Arnaut, yet must admit that "great poets are not necessarily good critics" and that "we cannot read Arnaut easily for pleasure." [15] Perhaps, among the critics of our own time, it is in Ezra Pound that we may most easily find the key to Dante's estimate of Arnaut. As early as 1920, but looking ahead to a new critical school, as Grandgent looks back and essentially speaks for nineteenth-century criticism (I do not mean that as a stricture) Pound writes: "And Arnaut was the best artist among the Provençals, trying the speech in new fashions, and bringing new words into writing, and making new blendings of words" [16] Dante saw him as a maker of words—this was a matter of great importance to a critic who had analyzed word types in his *De vulgari* and was to cry out for the *rime aspre e chioccie* (harsh and ugly rhymes) essential for a description of lowest Hell. Del Monte has passionately defended all of Arnaut's technical tricks, finding an "aesthetic exigency" even in the *caras rimas* and affirming that even the metrical innovations are *vincolate all'originalità sentimentale e alla singolarità espressiva e non si possono quindi ridurre ad ardimenti artificiosi* (linked to his emotional originality and to his expressive individuality and cannot therefore be dismissed as gestures of bold artfulness).[17] This is to claim more than most readers would concede, I think, but even if we cannot see the *originalità sentimentale*, in a sestina for example, as clearly as Del Monte, yet we may grant that the *singolarità espressiva*, the new words, the elaborate patterns are indeed the work of a remarkable *fabbro* and so may understand the admiration that Dante the "wordsmith" must have felt for a master craftsman. Grandgent speaks very properly of Dante's "gratitude" in this regard: I think it led him too far, and even Pound concedes that the art of Arnaut is not literature, but the basis of it is sound enough.

As for Dante's lines in Provençal, it may be said that even today there is considerable argument about the text; most editors are content with Vandelli's reading, but Sapegno, for one, has two variations of his own. Actually even the widest variations do not change the essential meaning of the Provençal, which is remarkably clear in grammar and construction and childishly simple in vocabulary. I cannot agree with Bowra that the passage takes off Arnaut's style. It has, to be sure, a few antitheses, a commonplace of poetic rhetoric, but there are no nine lines in the work of Arnaut himself so simple in form, substance, and vocabulary. Sapegno indeed makes the comment that the *pasada folor* (past folly) of which Arnaut speaks may well refer to his artificial style, among other things, and sees in the line *no me puesc ni vuoill a vos cobrire* (I cannot nor will not hide myself from you), an overt repudiation of the *trobar clus*, where the intent was precisely to "cover oneself" against common understanding.[18] I think Sapegno is right and that two statements can be made on that basis; first, that although it be paradoxical to find Arnaut repudiating the very style which had first made Dante admire him, yet Dante's Arnaut has in fact given up both the amatory and the linguistic attitudes of the historic Arnaut. And secondly, I think it follows that his simple language may fairly be read in connection with Dante's own anti-rhetorical protestation of Canto xxiv, beginning *Io mi son un che quando/ amor mi spira* (I am one who when inspired by love). If there is a message of autobiographical-critical commentary in this passage, it seems to me that Dante is telling us that he owes much to Arnaut's explorations of technique but also that he has not so much rejected as surpassed the obsession with it—as Arnaut in his new penitential illumination must also have done.

As is right and proper—and consistent as much with the less-crowded world and ampler scope of the *Paradiso* as the deference due to sainthood—Dante's celestial representative of the *gai saber* gets fuller treatment and is allowed more wordage than his colleagues in the lower realms. Folquet de Marseille, the sainted singer of the Heaven of Venus, is given in fact sixty-one lines as against thirteen for Bertran de Born and a mere eight for the self-effacing Arnaut. Further, although his own words begin with line 82, the six flattering lines which serve as Cunizza's introduction to him (describing him as a flashing jewel and assuring him of five hundred years of enduring fame) begin with line 37. He is in fact the dominant figure of his canto (Cunizza defends herself well, but has ten lines less assigned to her). His monologue covers a wide range of information and commentary. After telling Dante of his origins, his name, and his excessive devotion to love, he affirms, reinforcing Cunizza's complacent statement, that he looks back on such a life without regret, rejoicing only in the Providence *ch'ordinò e provide* (which ordained and provided). As another example of such Providence he calls Dante's attention to the effulgence of Rahab, his neighbor, and in the course of extolling her aid to Joshua goes on to criticize the Pope for not carrying on the Crusade to free the Holy Land. The Pontiff's negligence is in part the fault of the "accursed flower," the florin—of which Folquet, son of a merchant, must have had a better understanding than his brother troubadours—greed for which has corrupted the clergy, now more intent on the lucrative study of the Decretals than on the Gospels and the Annunciation. He ends by predicting that the Vatican will soon be free of this "adultery."

It is not hard to see why Dante chose Folquet for this high level of his occitanic delegation. Although he had been ruthless in his persecution of the Catharists, Folquet's very zeal made him the hero of the orthodox, and his conversion from poetry to the religious life must have aroused wonder and admiration in the faithful of his time. His association with the bloody Crusade has marred his image for modern readers: Scartazzini quotes approvingly Bartoli's phrase identifying Folquet as the *feroce vescovo, collegato ai crociati che andavano a distruggere la sua povera patria* (ferocious bishop, the ally of the Crusaders, who were going to destroy his poor country).[19] But quite aside from the fact that Languedoc was not the *patria* of a poet born in Marseilles of Genoese stock, it would be unfair to expect Dante in the context of his times to share our post-Reformation tenderness for the unfortunate Cathar-

ists. And in truth Stroński has assembled convincing evidence
of our Bishop's good reputation even among his enemies in
those trying days: he concludes, "*Homme d'une intelligence
supérieure et d'une activité prodigeuse . . . on le regardait
généralement comme un homme de caractère honnêt.*" [20] Add
to these virtues his secure place in the troubadour tradition
(Dante had already shown his awareness of it, giving laudatory
mention to a canto of Folquet's in *De vulgari* II, vi) and his
election to Heaven becomes predictable.

As far as his political attitudes are concerned Folquet has
undergone some readjustment at Dante's hands. The crusading zeal which comes out in his reproach to the lethargic and
venal papacy is authentic; aside from his own activities against
the Albigensians, Folquet, in his lyric youth, had written two
Crusade poems which survive: one for the Spanish struggle
against the Moors, the other on behalf of the Third Crusade in
outremer. But into the mouth of this staunch defender of or-
thodoxy and the papal right, Dante puts some of the harshest
words in the *Comedy* uttered against the conduct of the papacy, for surely "adultery" as a description of the condition of
the Church goes very far in its suggestion of illegality as well
as indecency.

Benvenuto thought the term applicable particularly to Boniface VIII, whose "marriage" to the Church was "adulterous"
in that the true "husband" was Celestinus, but, as various commentators have pointed out the link with the cognate verb
"avolterate" (*Inferno* XIX, 4) may suggest a less specific application. The "crusader" Folquet, we may well believe, spoke
with the same intensity but directed himself at a different tar-
get. Dante further somewhat alters the historical personage—
or at least the poet as we know him—by assigning to him a
greater depth of amorous commitment, a more unbridled
passion, in his youth than the extant poems would seem to
bear out. As compared to the sensualism of some of the verses
of William of Poitou and the dedicated avowals of Bernart de
Ventadorn, the love verses of Folquet seem rather mild and

conventional: *des réflexions laborieuses sur l'amour. . . . des tissus de motifs littéraires et de lieux communs* is Stroński's verdict.[21] But the greatest change the troubadour suffers is in the area of his style and language. Dante had admired his *canso, Tan m'abellis l'amoros pensamens* (So pleasing to me is the amorous thought), and indeed had exalted it as an example of the high style. He had borrowed the first three words on behalf of Arnaut Daniel, but Folquet gets the better of the exchange, for in the Heaven of Venus he speaks with a language more reminiscent of Arnaut's than any of the Provençal verses chanted in the refining fire. All commentators have remarked on the baroque circumlocution with which Folquet describes the city of his birth; it takes him in fact some eleven lines to state simply "I was born in Marseilles." He goes on with references to the daughter of Belus, "the Rhodopean maid deceived by Demophoön" and Alcides, none of whom appears in his own works. Although Dante uses very sparingly the *rime riche*, no less than three examples appear in Folquet's discourse (*torna, palma,* and *pianta*), and his entire speech is a web of periphrases. His rhetorical twin is Pier della Vigna; there is no other comparison that suggests itself (certainly not the chastened Arnaut), but the Bishop is much more erudite than the Imperial Secretary. It is true that Cunizza's vocabulary with its invented *s'incinqua*, its Latinisms *propinqua* and *luculenta*, and Dante's own neologisms, *s'inluia, intuassi, immii,* are of the same nature. Which is to say, I think, that the whole canto is a linguistic tribute to Folquet.

I cannot help thinking (and the thought may have occurred to others although I have noted no particular reference to it) that Folquet has replaced Guiraut de Bornelh as the Provençal representative of the poetry of rectitude (*De vulgari* II, ii). It is well known that Dante strove for consistency in his works, and, once having set down his theories on the proper subjects for lofty verse, there is no reason to assume that he did not continue to have them in mind and indeed to think that they could be exemplified from the Provençal (regrettably arms were still unsung by the Italians). And in fact two of his three examples mentioned in the *De vulgari* reappear in the *Comedy*. But what has become of Guiraut? When he wrote the *De vulgari* Dante had held Guiraut in unusually high esteem. "The Limousin" is quoted four times, more often than any other troubadour, quite aside from his identification with rectitude, the highest of Dante's categories. The citations are interesting in their implications. Although the first quotation is merely to illustrate the similarity of *amor* and *amore* in the two vernaculars, the second, referring to one of Guiraut's most admired *sirventes*, *Per solatz revelhar* (To restore good society), is apparently the best example of a song of "rectitude" that Dante can think of; the third is brought in to show the majesty of the eleven-syllable line, and the fourth, *Ar auziretz encabalitz cantars* (Now you will hear perfect songs), is held up as a model of "the most excellent degree of construction," having "flavor and grace and also elevation." In sensing a kindred spirit in Guiraut, Dante's intuition did not betray him. Chaytor finds Dante's choice of him as the poet of righteousness is "entirely justified by the high moral tone of his sirventes." [22] De Lollis pointed out that Guiraut's poetic fused most successfully *la materia amorosa e la morale* (the amatory and ethical substance),[23] which can also be said of the "moral *canzoni*"—*Le dolci rime* (The sweet rhymes), *Doglia mi reca* (Grief brings me), *Tre donne intorno al cor* (Three ladies round my heart), and *Poscia ch'amor* (Since love). Santangelo, pressing the findings of De Lollis to a logical conclusion, states that for Dante in 1305 Guiraut was the best of the troubadours, surpassing Arnaut even in amatory verse.[24]

What then has happened between 1305 and the year of *Purgatorio* XXVI? Santangelo sees in the exaltation of "rectitude" over love the refuge of a poet *povero e quasi mendico, disistimato dagli uomini, non calcolato dalle donne* (a pauper and almost a mendicant, held in scant esteem by men and ignored by women); later, the exile *non più vilipeso ma ben trattato e stimato* (no longer scorned but well treated and held in esteem) turned back to love and to the imitation of Arnaut in the *Petrose* and his exaltation in the *Purgatorio*.[25] Change of spirit and attitude there must have been, but I am not sure that it is of the sort that Santangelo has in mind, springing essentially from the material condition of the poet's life or the state of his prestige. I do not see so much a turning from *rectitudo* to *amor* as the development of a different concept of *rectitudo*. This would leave Arnaut unassailable as the champion of *amore*, but if *rectitudo* is still to be supreme—and if it is not supreme in the *Comedy* then the allegory is meaningless—it is going to need another and more suitable example than Guiraut. For it seems to me that the *rectitudo* Dante had in mind in the *De vulgari* was the kind of ethical virtue which one associates with the climate of the *Convivio* (of which the *De vulgari* may be regarded as an interpolation or an excursus, as Dante's own remarks indicate). And without going into the *selva oscura* of *Convivio* exegesis, it may fairly be pointed out that the inspiration of that noble work is essentially philosophical; Lady Philosophy openly displaces Beatrice. The rectitude of the *Convivio* seems to have little need of Revelation. In the *Comedy*, on the other hand, Revelation is Dante's guide. Guiraut, at least as Dante conceived of him, could have satisfied the requirements for the *Convivio-De vulgari* period, but, for a dweller in Paradise (the only proper eternal residence for a Christian poet of rectitude), he would not quite do, and an all-but-canonized Bishop, happily also a singer, was evidently preferable. Although possibly it is simply an indication of a change of taste (and Dante is never more firm in his judgments than when he has had occasion to change an opinion, as he reveals in Book II of the *De monarchia*), yet the disparagement of Guiraut in Canto XXVI of the *Purgatorio* may also be meant to prepare us for his displacement from his previous high rank and so to open the way for the intrusion of Folquet into the triad.

This substitution and glorification of the Bishop is underlined, it seems to me, by Dante's introduction of his new champion. Not only does Cunizza present him in glowing terms but Dante's intense curiosity to learn of his identity is unparalleled in the *Comedy*—only in the case of Ulysses does he show something of the same impatience.

And it is this pointed anticipation which gives us the ultimate key and supplies the full answer to why Dante chose Folquet for his climactic love poet. For, as in the *bolgia* of the false counselors he had realized that he was among souls who shared his gifts of intellectual distinction and thus could hardly wait to hear the master of many devices, so here, in Folquet, he sees a kindred spirit, a poet once consumed by love who has now put it behind him, and who, not repudiating but freely accepting his past, has yet moved on to higher concerns, still interested in the affairs of the world yet serene in his contemplation of his vision. Dante too has followed, in the brief phase of Apollonio, *l'itinerario di Folco dalla poesia alla religione* (Folquet's itinerary from poetry to religion).[26] For the creator of the *Comedy*, Folquet was inevitable. And for the pilgrim too, I believe we may hazard the guess that Folquet is the soul he expects to see. Cunizza's words are an indication that it must be a love poet, and her associations are with the Provençal; her phrase indicates that his five hundred years of fame have only begun—and Dante can make a shrewd guess as to who is enclosed in the jewel-like radiance. But he burns to be sure—and dramatizes his eagerness to underline the significance of his choice. The ultimate poet of love, also the poet of righteousness, and not unfamiliar with arms for that matter—such is Folquet. And the description would fit Dante Alighieri equally well.

With Folquet the Provençal trio is complete. But there is another poet of the *langue d'oc* who has a substantial role in the *Comedy*—even if his linguistic anomaly somewhat spoils the symmetry of the triangle. However, I do not think that Dante meant Sordello to "count" as a Provençal figure. I believe that, even as the poet of Goito ignores the Latinity of

Virgil and sees in him only a fellow Lombard, so Dante sees in Sordello not the Provençal poet but the Italian-born patriot and judge of princes. But the language of his verse (at least as we know it today) was the *langue d'oc*, and whether or not he is a part of the truly Provençal gallery we cannot leave him out of our considerations. Nor should we want to; his function, his aura, and his implications are well worth our study.

He is one of the important and impressive figures in the *Purgatorio*. His presence takes in three cantos: in Canto vi he springs up to embrace Virgil, incidentally inspiring Dante's famous invective; in Canto vii he leads our pilgrims to the vale of the princes and points out with comment the ranking dignitaries in that crepuscular conclave, concluding with remarks on inherited virtues or, rather, the lack of them. In Canto viii he calls attention to the coming of the serpent. He is a true guide (in the sense of leading our poets from one place to another), an informant, a commentator, and clearly, since his gesture touches off the aforesaid invective, an inspiration.

Obviously Dante must have had a high opinion of the warrior troubadour. But does his Sordello in fact have very much in common with the Sordello of history? Many have chosen to emphasize the differences between the lion of the mountainside and the adventurer of Goito: *Certo il Sordello di Dante non è, come oggi si ripete comunemente, il Sordello che scrisse il celebre serventese in morte di ser Blacatz . . . il Sordello ritratto da Dante non è il giudice impavido dei potenti* (Certainly the Sordello of Dante is not, as is commonly repeated nowadays, the Sordello who wrote the famous *sirventes* on the death of Lord Blacatz . . . the Sordello depicted by Dante is not the intrepid judge of the mighty), Gentile affirms.[27] I would be inclined to argue that he is indeed just that—yet not by any means the historical Sordello either. The facts of our troubadour's life, such as they are (and we know more about him than we do about many of his colleagues), have been summarized by his recent editor, Marco Boni, with all the up-to-date findings of scholarship at his disposal. To summarize the ninety pages dedicated to his subject's biography, we may hold it as reasonably certain that Sordello was born in Goito near Mantua, a scion of the lesser nobility, probably in the last years of the twelfth century. After a gay and carefree youth, given to the study of the troubadours' art (and somewhat to gambling), he created a scandal by eloping with Cunizza, wife of Ricciardo di San Bonifazio and sister of Ezzelino da Romano (who seems to have instigated the abduction for political reasons of his own). There is an allusion to another liaison and then (*circa* 1226) came the departure for Provence. Many years in the court of Raymond Berenger IV followed and, on the death of that lord and the marriage of his daughter to Charles of Anjou, Sordello entered the latter's service. He returned to Italy with his ambitious and fortunate master, may have fought at Benevento, and was rewarded by the bestowal of various fiefs, including the castle of Palena (Abruzzi) with all its adjuncts. This in 1269, after which no more is heard of the poet.[28]

Essentially all this information is contained in the two Provençal biographies of the poet, and it seems not at all unlikely that Dante was well-acquainted with such facts. Did he know more than we do? Or at least more than twentieth-century scholarship would like to guarantee? This question may be asked specifically with regard to two matters affecting the Sordello of the mountainside; one perhaps relatively trivial, the other more important for our assessment of the troubadour. As to the first question, it is connected with the place assigned to Sordello on the mount. As we meet him he stands alone, like Saladin, as numerous commentators have pointed out. But Dante's categories are firm and permit of few unassigned casuals. We must therefore ask: are we to think of Sordello as belonging to the previous group (those who met death by violence and repented only at the last minute), or is the troubadour himself to be thought of as one of the "negligent" princes whom he later joins? Or is he—quite exceptionally—*sui generis*? If we are to assign him to the preceding group, then we must assume that he met with a violent death and that Dante was aware of this circumstance. Benvenuto is the first of the commentators to suggest any such possibility, and his account has the color more of fiction than fact. Yet some scholars, such as Anglade and Marigo, have accepted the likelihood of Sordello's coming to a violent end; others, less certain of the fact, believe that Dante thought so—Torraca, Santangelo, and, among commentators, Casini Barbi.[29] And I think the question can best be resolved not by refutation of Benvenuto's account but by simple examination of the text. In line 25 Dante speaks of being "free of all those souls" who are crowding in on him to ask for his prayers and so gives the clear impression of leaving that group definitely behind him. Nor does he immediately meet Sordello. In line 28 he begins with Virgil a discussion on the efficacy of prayer, and this digression in the narrative takes up thirty lines; it is not until line 58 that Virgil calls his attention to the brooding Lombard poet. This, it seems to me, clearly marks Sordello off from the preceding group of souls. Furthermore, although he stands at first above them so that Dante may better study their aspects, yet he does finally join them (VIII, 43–44: *Or avvalliamo omai/ tra le grandi ombre*—Now let us descend/ among the great shades) *come in sua propria dimora . . . o perchè principe anch'esso . . . o almeno frequentatore di Corti, come ci è ricordato dalla storia, o meglio, qual giudice, anche in vita, di azioni e costumi principeschi* (as if into his proper dwelling . . . either because he too was a prince or at least a courtier, as history records, or perhaps better in his capacity, in life too, as judge of the actions and customs of princes).[30] As for his forming a *parte per se stesso* (a party by himself), although this is the view of Sapegno (and, earlier, Porena), I cannot see much to be said for it; there is no case of Dante's making a category for one soul alone in all of the *Comedy* (even Satan has company of a sort), nor would it be easy, in Sordello's case, to say just what such a category would be. Those who remark the verbal similarity between the descriptions of him and Saladin—*E solo in una parte vidi il Saladino/ . . . un'anima, che posta/ sola soletta* (alone in one place I saw Saladin/ . . . a soul placed all alone)—might remember that Saladin too, though he stood alone, was part of a well-defined and fairly numerous category.

But the more arresting second question which has been asked in this connection is whether Dante thought of Sordello as an Italian writer and specifically whether he had knowledge of any of the poet's compositions in his native tongue. The mention of Sordello in the *De vulgari* is couched in rather obscure language. In discussing the speech of Bologna and its relative excellence Dante says that its beauty may owe something to the fact that it borrows a little from neighboring towns. He goes on to say, *sicut facere quoslibet a finitimis suis conicimus, ut Sordellus de Mantua sua ostendit, Cremone, Brixie atque Verone confini; qui, tantus eloquentie vir existens, non solum in poetando, sed quomodocunque loquendo patrium vulgare deseruit* (just as we conjecture that all borrow from their neighbors, as Sordello showed with respect to his own Mantua, which is adjacent to Cremona, Brescia, and Verona; and he who was so distinguished by his eloquence not only in poetry, but in every other form of utterance forsook his native vulgar tongue).[31] (*De vulgari* I, xv, 2). I believe the best gloss on this is that of Ferrers Howell, who paraphrases the passage as follows: "The reasoning by which the relative superiority of the Bologna dialect is established is less clearly expressed than is usual with Dante. The following free paraphrase is submitted as a plausible explanation of this difficult passage. 'The peoples of every city borrow from their neighbours, and their dialects are better or worse (from the literary point of view) according to the character resulting from the mixture of the borrowed elements with the original speech. Hence the superiority of the Bologna dialect: for though the sharpness borrowed from Ferrara and Modena is bad in itself, it mixes well with the smoothness and softness borrowed from Imola. The same truth is illustrated as regards Mantua by the case of Sordello. The dialect of this place is bad, because of the badness of the elements borrowed from Cremona, Brescia, and Verona. Sordello, in fact, after some literary attempts in this dialect, found it so unsuitable that he forsook his native tongue entirely, wrote exclusively in Provençal, and became a Provençal to all intents and purposes.' " [32] Marigo, following Zingarelli, believes that the *quomodocunque loquendo* (every other form of utterance) must allude to formal speeches composed in a language free from traces of dialect and only wishes some specimen of Sordello's Italian poetry were extant.[33] Bertoni in fact thought that he had found one and published it,[34] and Boni, though somewhat hesitantly and only *in appendice*, prints the verses and is not entirely prepared to deny their authenticity.[35] However one may read the rather ambiguous sentence of the *De vulgari*, the suggestion is certainly present that Dante knew of some kind of Italian work written by Sordello. Indeed, for the champion of Italian unity, for the symbol of a lofty *patriottismo dell'amore e della pace* (Gentile)—patriotism of love and peace—I think such a hypothesis is essential.

Yet the recognizable source of Sordello's commentary on the princes is certainly the celebrated lament for Blacatz. D'Ancona notes that even the scheme of Dante's survey follows that of the *planh sirventes*; on the mountainside, as in life, Sordello, feudal spirit that he is, begins with the Emperor and works down to the lesser nobility. It has been remarked too that one prince, Henry III of England, appears in both compositions, the kind of linkage that would be, I think, characteristic of Dante. I believe too the lament is also present in another part of the Sordello episode. Dante's own invective, deploring the state of Italy and lashing out against those who are responsible for it, has similar emotional ingredients; Sapegno in fact says it is an *invettiva* (invective) which is also a *compianto* (lament)—which is merely to Italianize the Provençal term *planh sirventes*.

Was Dante also familiar with Sordello's 1,314-line didactic work, the *Ensenhamen*, which contained rules, ethical and social, for good conduct and correct manners—a kind of medieval *cortegiano* designed to teach us *de far be et de vivre gen* (to do good and live well, line 403)? If and how well Dante knew this composition would be hard to say. Torraca believed he saw an echo of some lines of the work in *Inferno* III, 34 ff.,[36] and Boni seems willing to agree;[37] Guarnerio's suggestion that *Paradiso* VI, 131–132, are a like echo is a little more daring.[38] Recently Bowra has attempted to show that Dante's invective parallels the contents of the *Ensenhamen*.[39] It is true that such topics as the wickedness of the rich, the degeneration of the times, and the nobility of character as against that of birth suggest the moralizing Dante of the *Convivio;* they also suggest any number of medieval treatises, including some in Provençal. It would be hard to establish any real connection between the *Ensenhamen* and the contents of Cantos VI and VII. But I do think that Dante may have been familiar with the *Ensenhamen* and certainly knew that Sordello had composed such a work. For it must have been, I believe, a contributing element in building up Dante's high opinion of a figure whose presence in our poet's gallery of heroes would be otherwise hard to explain.

Sordello had not only abducted Cunizza, he had bragged, in a composition that we may hope is of his early years, of success at "lady-killing" (the phrase is his) and had issued fair warning to all husbands of his prowess in this area.[40] Italian though he was, he had spent thirty-five years of his life in the service (apparently happy) of foreign princes; he had returned to Italy in the train of the arch-enemy of Dante's empire, a fighting Guelph. It is hard to see how this record could have appealed to Dante. Flamini suggested years ago that Dante might have been acquainted with the aged Cunizza;[41] if she was in her old age willing to "indulge herself" as she was in Heaven, she may well have been willing to indulge the memory of her youthful abductor and (so they said) lover. We know that Dante thought well of Cunizza in the teeth of the *vulgo,* and perhaps Sordello creeps into *Purgatorio* under her mantle. Perhaps too, Guelph or not, he inspired Dante's respect as an example of a poet who had also achieved success and dignity in military and political affairs—*era divenuto cavaliere nobile e austero e consigliere dei principi e gran signore* (he had become a noble and austere knight, adviser of princes, and a great lord), as Viscardi has it.[42] The exiled Dante would have heard something of Sordello's prominence in the courts of Northern Italy, as Boni suggests. But for the appellation *tantus eloquentie vir* (man so great in eloquence), something more would have been necessary; the *Ensenhamen* is precisely the kind of work that would have drawn such a comment from Dante.

I find the real puzzle lies in Dante's association of the Lombard troubadour with national patriotism. There is nothing which could be called patriotic in the *Ensenhamen*, and the *planh sirventes* is, when carefully analyzed, merely the usual incitement to princes to fight for honor and their right. To be sure, the poet speaks out boldly to the great ones of the world (this too was common enough; troubadours, like jesters, were privileged characters), but his intent is clearly that of Bertran de Born's, to *mesclar los baros*, to stir up discord—and for the same reason: all the minor nobility and their hangers-on found in warfare their best chance for advancement and booty, and Sordello in fact did very well out of it. But of patriotism there is no trace. Here we can only say that Dante, having found in Sordello a figure to admire, a fellow poet (and some critics have seen in some of his verses a kind of adumbration of the *dolce stil nuovo*),[43] a companion of princes and a moralist—in short, someone much like himself—simply made the last leap and attributed to Sordello his own passionate concern for the unity of Italy and that *patriottismo dell'amore e della pace* which burned in his own breast.

Sordello's correspondences within the *Comedy* are rich in implication. His personal associations are with Cunizza and Ezzelino. It is a kind of personal triumvirate, with representation in all the realms somewhat similar to the imperial trio of

Frederick, Manfred, and Constance, or the Florentine clan of Piccarda, Forese, and (by 1308) Corso Donati. In his lion-like aloofness and his aggressive conversational approach he reminds us of Farinata. Gentile has noted the verbal signal in Virgil's *Vedi là*—"see there" (*Inf.* x, 31 and *Purg.* vi, 58) and quite rightly too, for they both symbolize deep political attachments; one to clan or faction (*Chi fur li maggior tui?*— Who were your forebears?) and the other to native country (*di nostro paese . . . c'inchiese*—he asked us about our country). But his figural correspondences are even richer. The garden of the princes is the *amoenus locus* corresponding to the Limbo of the *Inferno*; Virgil's terzina (*Purg.* vii, 25–30) underlines that, lest it should escape us, even as line 25, *non per far ma per non far* (not for deed but for omission), indicates the "negligence" that the two groups have in common. (It is to be noted, however, that the garden here contains only political figures and lacks the poet's philosophers and scientists of the Limbo—perhaps we should expect to find such only across the little stream of eloquence, and here there is no little stream.) And so some have seen him as corresponding to Virgil, who leads Dante to Limbo; D'Ancona has noted the Virgilian echo in vii, 40. Looking more closely, however, the actual leading to the castle where the great souls are surveyed is not Virgil's work; he seems to be led himself—or at least merely to go along as one of the group. Dante's line (*Inf.* iv, 103) *così andammo* (so we went) gives no indication of who leads, but surely it must be Homer, who has first saluted Virgil and must have an accepted position of pre-eminence among the escorting poets. This correspondence is high honor for Sordello, but if Homer knew better than any other poet the heroes of old and their virtues, who could know better than the author of the *planh* for Blacatz the merits and weaknesses of contemporary kings? His rôle may in fact invite comparison with even loftier characters. Like Cato he gives topographical directions, information on the by-laws of Purgatory, and some higher indoctrination as well. We may see him as a matching figure, the second warden as it were of the ante-Purgatory: Cato meets our pilgrims as they enter this realm of the tentative, and Sordello sees them depart. Verbal connection may be seen in the *solo* of Cato and the *anima soletta* of Sordello. We may recall that *soletta* is also descriptive of Matelda as she confronts the emancipated Dante across Lethe. One can make too much, I think, of these verbal echoes, but since Matelda too is guide and informant for Dante and leads him, as Sordello does, to another and even more glorious assembly of great spirits, we may be justified in seeing an intended clue in the repetition of this word (which appears a scant four times in the *Comedy*). Lastly, another venerable and intercessory figure comes to mind who is to display for Dante a supreme gallery—St. Bernard. An abyss lies between them, and the gallery of princes is a poor enough prefiguring of the pillars of the Church. Yet the suggestion, I think, is there, and Sordello points forward to the Rose even as he does backward to the fair castle and the virtuous spirits of Limbo. The flesh and blood of the soldier-troubadour are there, in his pose, in his assurance, in his unprejudiced survey of contemporary rulers, but Dante has given him stature and significance, indeed true grandeur in what he symbolizes and what, in the context of the sacred poem, he suggests.

7
Paradiso IX

&

Few would argue that the ninth canto of the *Paradiso* is the most beautiful or even the richest of the thirty-three cantos of the heavenly kingdom. A canto whose burden is chiefly political and hence lacking in that kind of philosophical-allegorical substance which has become the necessary manna of the twentieth-century critic, a canto lacking a principal character, almost devoid of truly beautiful lines, offering few textual problems (those enticing tidbits for the teeth of commentators old and new, *non ricco di singolari bellezze estetiche*—not rich in singular aesthetic points of beauty—as Flamini describes it),[1] it can scarcely claim on any account to present itself as one of the great cantos of the *Commedia*. Yet even as the heavenly bodies themselves are so disposed that "the parts shed splendor each on each," so every canto of the divine poem has its own special illumination without which the interchange of poetic light would be incomplete. If for no other reason, we should have to respect our canto for the position it holds: it concludes Dante's exploration of the third heaven and it marks also the end of the stage of his celestial journey which lies still under the earth's shadow. And before proceeding to a detailed analysis of the text, I should like to suggest too that in an overall consideration three aspects of the canto stand out, which, in their interplay and for their implications, justify its claim on the reader's interest. If we meet no Piccarda nor Cacciaguida, yet the characters that appear to the poet are memorable for what they say and significant, not merely symbolically, for what they are; certain linguistic devices the poet almost aggressively forces on us have implications that merit our attention; and the structure of the canto, which might at first sight appear a weakness, will yield, I believe, rewarding insight into Dante's sense of form and harmony.

The canto may be divided roughly into three parts: the final remarks of Charles Martel and his leave-taking (lines 1–12), the appearance of the three souls exemplifying the moral and doctrinal lessons of the canto (lines 13–126), and the apocalyptic prophecy directed against Florence and the clergy which concludes the canto (127–142). But in considering the weight that Dante has given to the individual figures, we should perhaps do greater justice to the poet's intention if we subdivided the middle division and considered the work as having five sections, as follows: (i) Charles Martel (1–12); (ii) Cunizza (13–66); (iii) Folquet (67–108); (iv) Rahab (109–126); (v) invective and prophecy (127–142). This gives us a pattern of some symmetry, and we may note in passing that both the prelude and the coda contain prophecies framing and underlining the political content of the messages of Cunizza and Folquet. A certain formal harmony is not wanting. If we look at the canto thematically, however, we may see a flaw, or what would be a flaw if the poet had conceived of the canto as a separate unit. For in substance the first division belongs properly to Canto VIII, rounding out as it does the figure of Charles Martel, which Dante has deliberately chosen to magnify in this way.

One is tempted to digress here and comment on the interplay of the formal and thematic patterns of the *Comedy*. There are cases, more frequently in the *Inferno* than in the other *cantiche*, where the formal unity of the canto is reinforced by the thematic unity of the argument. There are cases —the example of *Inferno* XXI–XXII comes readily to mind—

where two cantos, that is, formal units, cover one theme. With similar respect for the formal unity, though in reverse operation, *Inferno* XVIII covers three successive topical units. And there are other cases where the argument carries over from one canto to another, and the formal unit is all but submerged. I believe, in a purely technical sense, that the variations of relationship between cantos and subject matter are a great part of Dante's success as a craftsman. I am sure that he was quite aware, as are we who read, that to make each canto self-contained would have undermined the integrity of the work as a whole; conversely, to have made the canto division purely arbitrary in all cases would have signified the loss of the esthetic advantage which derives from respect for the structure of the work.

Leaving aside such larger considerations and returning to our subject, it seems to me clearly evident that in allowing Canto VIII to intrude as it were on the domain of Canto IX, Dante, aside from the compliment to Charles Martel, is indicating that the formal unity here is less significant than the transcendent unity of the heavenly order. It is the unity of the star that matters rather than that of the canto. Yet the canto has its function, and two such formal divisions contain the Heaven of Venus, the somewhat blurred frontier between them making the subdivisions (truly not unrelated) of the social instruction of Charles and the political-doctrinal message of Cunizza and Folquet.

Finally, this canto affords us an unusual opportunity to study our poet in his role of grammarian and word-maker. The author of *De vulgari eloquentia* could never be free of linguistic preoccupations. The manipulation of words is a major concern of any poet, but Dante's interest in words was scholarly as well as poetical: he did not merely select and employ words with care; he created them. Did he not—albeit in rather puzzling fashion—stress the linguistic bond between Virgil and Ulysses on the one hand and Dante and Guido da Montefeltro on the other, deep in the Malebolge? Did he not

plead for—and obtain—the *rime aspre e chiocce* (harsh and
ugly rhymes) suitable for a treatment of the ice-bound depths
of Hell? We need hardly be surprised if in the light of Paradise his linguistic inventiveness surpasses itself and breaks the
bondage of earthly speech, even as the laws of human nature
and science are transcended in that realm where "law of nature has no relevance." And surely nowhere in the poem is
Dante's linguistic daring more evident than here: in the ornate
speech of Folquet, the remarkable vocabulary of Cunizza, and
the bold creation of the verbs *inluiare, intuare, inmiare*, which
spring from the poet's own enraptured tongue. Following on
the persuasive dialectic of Charles Martel, such devices remind
us that we are in truth in the heaven of rhetoric.

Of the characters chosen (by God or by the poet) to appear in this canto we shall have more to say. Here we shall
observe that their rôle is not merely to set forth appropriate
dogmatic sentences and warn of earthly errors, but also,
within the plan of the poem, to contribute their thread to certain great bonds which unite the three parts of the *Comedy*.
One of the functions of the *Paradiso* is to résumé what has
been experienced and learned in the preceding *cantiche*; to this
end Cunizza and Folquet have been most artfully selected.

But let us now examine our text:

> After your Charles, fair Clemence, had made clear
>   Such things to me, he spoke of treacheries
>   His issue was yet destined to endure;
> But added: "Peace, and let the years roll on,"
>   So I say only that befitting tears
>   Will follow on the traces of your woes.
>
>   (1–6)

The magnanimity of Charles is unobtrusively stressed in his
postponing, as he does, the recital of the wrongs which his
stock was to suffer until his objective and altruistic discussion
of social misdirection has been completed. These wrongs—
which were in truth serious for a feudal monarch, for his

brother Robert usurped the throne of Naples (1309), de-
priving Carlo Roberto, son of our Charles, of his legitimate
inheritance—can now be seen in the illumination of Paradise
as merely another incident in the human record of injustice.
Charles no longer thinks first of his own suffering. Yet—we
are still in the earth's shadow—if resentment is dead, there is
still solemn satisfaction, not entirely impersonal, in the
thought of ultimate vindication which the turning years must
bring. Two minor puzzles confront us in these opening lines:
the identity of "fair Clemence" and the occasion of the "befitting tears" (line 5). On the first point, the older commentators
are divided, some opting for Clemence of Hapsburg, Charles's
wife, and others for his daughter of the same name, later wife
of Louis X of France. At first glance the apostrophe of the
poet would seem to be addressed to someone still living, and
since Charles's wife died in 1295 it would seem likely that
Dante is addressing the daughter. On the other hand, nothing
in the text compels us to believe that "fair Clemence" is anything more than a device of chivalrous rhetoric intended to
honor the person addressed, whether living or dead, while the
possessive "your" would seem certainly more applicable to a
wife than a daughter. Momigliano and more recently Sapegno,
to cite the most modern of acute commentators, both invoke
Del Lungo, first to see in the "your" an "essentially conjugal
appellation," in support of their identification of Clemence as
the wife; and indeed the reader untroubled by knowledge of
chronology would assuredly so take it.[2]

As for the prophecy, some, beginning with Pietro di
Dante, have seen in it an allusion to the battle of Montecatini
(29 August 1315) in which Uguccione della Faggiuola de-
feated the Florentines and their Neapolitan allies; it is sure that
the usurper Robert lost a brother and a nephew on this occasion, but as these were also kinsmen of Charles Martel's the
vengeance would seem rather ambiguous. In truth, as Sapegno
suggests, if Dante had had this battle in mind (and if it had
taken place when he wrote these lines) we might have ex-

pected a more specific reference.³ I am inclined to think that the "befitting tears" may not be of this world at all; if they are we may well say with Scartazzini, "since the poet has said nothing it is pointless to make guesses concerning the actual facts to which he may be alluding." It seems to me too that the princely and benign character of Charles Martel, as we have seen it displayed, would lose nothing of its lofty nature in the contemplation of God's future justice; it might however be somewhat tarnished if we read into it the vindictive satisfaction at the death of a kinsman. It is on a note of serene almost distant contentment that Charles takes his leave, followed by Dante's melancholy comment:

> Already had that saintly splendor's life
> Turned to the Sun that keeps it ever full,
> Being a bounty ample for all needs.
> Ah souls deceived and creatures impious,
> Who turn your hearts away from such a Good,
> Raising your temples up in vanity!
>
> (7–12)

"Life" (line 7) in the sense of "soul" is so used for the first time in the *Paradiso;* the original *tanto* (line 9) in the sense of "sufficient," "adequate," is also a somewhat unusual meaning for the word according to Buti. Charles, having, as it were, condescended to human contact and to a discussion of earthly affairs, returns to his joyous contemplation of things eternal. The rhythm of the terzina, no less than its substance, depicts for us the comforting languor of such self-surrender. In terzina 10–12 we may see not only a general moral and quasi-mystical exhortation, but also a faint echo of the didactic passage with which Canto VIII had terminated; *torcete* (turn) is in fact repeated and surely not without purpose. Even as in higher things the "impious creatures" misdirect their hearts, so in the management of the practical affairs of the world, whose essence is in education, individuals are misdirected in their life employment. Thus the concern for human affairs (the earth's shadow) is again underlined even as Charles returns to his true home.

Dante and the reader have scant time to ponder such implications for, with the unselfish spontaneity of love, another splendor appears to claim the poet's attention:

> Behold, another of those splendors came
> Toward me and, waxing outwardly more bright,
> Revealed his eagerness to bring me joy.
> The eyes of Beatrice, as before
> Firm fixed on me with fond assent, bestowed
> Assurance in expressing my desire.
> "Pray grant swift correspondence"—so I spoke—
> "To what I seek, blest spirit; give evidence
> That what I think I can reflect in you."
>
> (13–21)

These transitional verses, aside from reinforcing in the reader's mind the picture of a Dante eager to greet the souls of Paradise and taking an almost childlike joy in their splendor, subject always to Beatrice's consent, serve also as a necessary interval between two scenes and two dialogues. Dante had swiftly become aware of Cunizza (not knowing yet who she is), but to have been presented abruptly would have been unworthy of her—and would have occasioned too hasty a dismissal of Charles Martel. So the formula of obtaining Beatrice's consent consumes a terzina and the address to the spirit yet another. And the reader suffers just enough suspense during these courteous preliminaries to realize that one not unworthy of Charles's heaven is about to speak. So much greater, then, the shock—to Dante's contemporaries—when her identity is disclosed.

> Whereat that light, which was still new to me,
> Out of its deeper part whence sprang its song
> Resumed as one rejoicing to do well.
> "Within that region of the wicked land
> Of Italy, between Rialto lying

> And sources of the Brenta and Piave,
> There stands a hill, rising not over high
> Whence on a time a firebrand came down
> To ravage all the country round about.
> Of that same torch's root I sprang, Cunizza
> I was called and here I scintillate
> Because this planet's life held me enthralled.
> Yet joyfully within me I approve
> The occasion of my lot, which irks me not;
> This might seem hard for your herd to believe."
>
> (22–36)

Cunizza, as becomes a member of a noble family, mentions first the region whence she had sprung (the *Marca Trevisana* is here "bounded" in a few lines beautiful for the poetry of their place names) and then the head of her house. The "hill" of line 28 is the "hill of Romano," whence Cunizza's clan derived its name. Similarly, to cite one of many cases: "I was from Montefeltro, I am Bonconte" (*Purg.* v, 88). And we may recall Farinata's question was not "Who are you?" but "Who were your forebears?" The phraseology of lines 25–30 not only indicates that an aristocrat is speaking but subtly links Cunizza with the gallery of noble figures—perhaps we can call this the Ghibelline thread—whom Dante has met in the course of his journey. Another link is suggested by the phrase, "wicked land of Italy," recalling the "our wicked land" of Jacopo Rusticucci (*Inf.* xvi, 9). As in the *girone* of the violent so here the phrase reveals not only an indignant sadness on the part of the speaker (as yet unidentified in both cases) for the affairs of a mortal world still held dear, but, in its very denunciatory force, also a moral rectitude (at least in public matters). Nor is this verbal memory of Hell out of place; it prepares us for the allusion to Ezzelino, Cunizza's brother, whom we saw submerged up to the *pelo così nero* (hair so black) in the blood bath of the Phlegethon (*Inf.* xii, 109). The ferocity of Ezzelino had been noteworthy even in a ferocious century; "the most cruel and feared lord that ever was among Christians," on the word of Villani. Legend added picturesque details: it was said that he was covered all over with black hair (hence the *pelo nero*) and that a devil inhabited his body; in very truth the chronicler told of his refusal to accept the last rites of the Church.[4] It is Pietro di Dante who tells the tale (similar to the one told of St. Dominic by Dante and by Boccaccio of Dante himself) of Ezzelino's mother who *dum partui eius esset vicina, somniabat quod parturiebat unam facem igneam, quae comburebat totam Marchiam Trevisanam* (when she was about to give birth, dreamed that she would bring forth a firebrand which would consume the entire March of Treviso). But I do not think Dante has chosen the image solely because of the tale; its infernal and destructive fire serves as an introduction, contrast, and in a sense a reinforcement of Cunizza's "I scintillate" (*refulgo*). For in truth a fiery glow surrounds both brother and sister, unholy in the one, saintly now in the other. The *Ottimo Commento* has noted how the contrasting temperaments—and different eternal destinations—of this pair exemplify the remarks of Charles Martel on human inheritance.[5] But if we may now describe the sister as saintly, it was not always so, for the earthly fire in which Cunizza had lived for years was of the same nature as that which had scorched the luckless Francesca, to whom our memory must also return as we contemplate love purified and triumphant in Paradise. The world, and not merely the *vulgo*, might more easily have condemned the Trevisana than the unsuspecting bride of Gianciotto. Cunizza had in fact led a life of no less notoriety than her brother. Born in 1198 and still alive in 1279, her amorous vicissitudes had been numerous: she had had three husbands (Ricciardo di San Bonifazio, Lord of Verona, Almerico di Braganza, and a gentleman of Verona not otherwise identified); she had been twice abducted—apparently quite willingly—by different lovers, the most celebrated being Sordello, with whom she lived in illicit happiness for several years;[6] and of her further adventures Lana tells us: "that she was so generous with her love that she would have thought it churlish to refuse anyone who had requested it with courtesy." But if she is ready to grant herself happy indulgence it has not been so with all the commentators; Scartazzini, as we have seen, found it difficult to understand why Dante put her in Heaven.

Since Cunizza, old and presumably penitent, died in Florence during the poet's youth, in her testament giving freedom to her bondsmen, it may be that the impression the young Dante had of her was such as to make him anxious to grant her salvation.[7] (I doubt that she is here simply or even primarily because she is particularly appropriate as a prophetess of Guelph disasters, though such considerations may have had their weight.) She is here, I believe, primarily as Francesca is in Hell, to illustrate by an extreme case a point of dogma. In a way we may see in Francesca-Cunizza a sort of amorous feminine Guido-Bonconte. One act damns Francesca because her hour had come and repentance was impossible; yet a lifetime in which reason has been persistently subjected to desire counts as nothing against the true penance, which, given time by God's inscrutable wisdom, Cunizza was able to offer. And so in an Augustinian sense[8] she may well congratulate herself [9] —and there is a certain complacency in the rhythm and the music as well as the substance of line 34—on the course of her life, which, whatever it may have seemed to the herd, had brought her safe to shore.

But perhaps we can go a little beyond the dogma. Cunizza was *lasciva* but not all evil; Benvenuto, allowing her to be *recte filia Veneris* (a true daughter of Venus), yet speaks of her also as *pia, benigna, misericors, compatiens miseris* (pious, kind, merciful, compassionate towards the wretched. We have remarked on the humanity of her last testament, and does not even the satirical comment of Lana betoken a certain generosity of soul? One is tempted to see in Cunizza an openhearted largeness of spirit that may at once tolerate and extenuate worse sins than lust. Anything but scrupulous or austere, she did not weigh the sins of the flesh heavily; "she indulged herself cheerfully" perhaps even in her lifetime, but to have been kind, merciful, compassionate towards the wretched—at a time and in a world where "pride, envy, and avarice" reigned supreme, this was no small virtue. Was even the sweet Francesca merciful and compassionate towards the wretched, we wonder—and since she speaks only of her own tragedy we shall never know. God knew and His judgment cannot err. Surely the complacency of Cunizza, to which we have referred, her candid delight in finding herself among the saved, bespeaks an innocent, almost childlike character.

Aside from her exemplification of dogma and her own distinction as a personality, this serene lady well fulfills the function of a paradisiacal figure in sending the reader's mind ranging over the *Comedy*, in making him aware of how tightly the threads of the great tapestry are woven. For Cunizza is not only sister to Ezzelino and in another sense to Francesca, dwellers in Hell; she is also associated with Sordello of the *Purgatorio* (surely an association that in part explains why Dante chose her); she is a Ghibelline lady (like Constance) and, contemplating her political interests, we call to mind Farinata, who also fought for the Empire, and Manfred, who, like her, has his quarrel with a partisan cleric. And she is further, thanks to the *lume d'esta stella* (light of this star), a citizen of love's domain and belongs no less to the realm of poetry than to that of politics. Whom better than Sordello's lady could Dante have chosen to present the one troubadour who is also a saint? Though eager to disclose to Dante the travails ordained for the wicked land, she cannot forbear to indicate, in verses which reflect her own modesty and carry a preliminary savor of the rhetoric which we are to hear from Folquet, that a soul much greater than she stands beside her.

> Of the bright sparkling and precious gem
> Of this our heaven, standing nearest me
> Great fame survives below and ere it die
> This hundredth year shall yet be quintupled.

> See now how men should practice to excell
> So one life may leave after it another.
>
> (37–42)

Verses rich in linguistic fantasy; *luculenta* (bright sparkling) appears here for the first time in the *Comedy*;[10] *propinqua* (near) adds with its Latinism a touch of classic solemnity
to a purely factual statement; and lines 40 and 42 are so elabo-
rately constructed as to call for interpretation by all the
commentators. The majority take line 40, with its newly
coined verb *s'incinqua* (literally, enfives itself) to signify that
the fame of Folquet has yet another five hundred years to run.
(Probably our poet, in common with all his contemporaries,
expected the Second Coming at about that time.)[11] As for line
42, we may agree with Momigliano that "one life" refers to
the terrestrial, "another" to the heavenly. And clearly, since
the saintly name of Folquet is past all mortal measurement, it is
earthly fame rather than eternal glory that Cunizza has in
mind. For a moment the values of Heaven are put aside and
the lesson of the saint echoes the Virgilian praise of fame (*Inf.*
XXIV, 49–51). Folquet, in company with God's athlete, had
striven mightily on earth (and perhaps Cunizza, "love-en-
thralled" herself, has in mind also his accomplishments as a
poet) and has his own reward in earthly as in eternal terms. But
the crass and perverse "horde" has lost sight of this goal, as it
has of the higher one.

> No such thought moves the horde which nowadays
> The Tagliamento and the Adige
> Enclose, nor beaten will it yet repent . . .
>
> (43–45)

A certain aristocratic disdain, not entirely unexpected in a
Ghibelline lady, though a little surprising in one of God's
saints, is apparent in the use of the word *turba* (horde) echoing the *vulgo* of line 36. Cunizza is no democrat; the mass as
such has no appeal for her and from her present eminence and

propinquità the inhabitants of her homeland are a horde of undistinguished and all but anonymous rogues. Such fame as they may claim is the perverted *fama* of misdeeds and follies; not even defeat will teach them the error of their ways. And leaving the past and the general to treat of the specific and the future, Cunizza gives warning of three tragic events yet to befall the stubborn folk of her march.

> But Padua soon will alter at the Marsh
> The water flowing by Vicenza's walls,
> So boorish to their duty are her folk.
> And where Cagnan bears Sile company
> One struts the lord and goes with head held high
> For whose betrayal now the web is spun.
> Feltro shall yet bemoan the treachery
> Of its disloyal pastor—act so foul
> That none has entered Malta for the like.
> Of vast capacity would be the vat
> Apt to receive all the Ferrara blood
> —And weary he who'd weigh it ounce by ounce—
> That this obliging priest will offer up
> To prove his politics; this sort of gift
> Will suit the style of living in yon parts.
>
> (46–60)

In 1314 Can Grande, going to the aid of Vicenza under attack from the Paduans ("boorish"—that is, rebellious to their duty to the Emperor, whose vicar Can Grande was), inflicted (12 September) on the latter such a defeat as to cause the marshes of the Bacchiglione River in the environs of Vicenza to run with blood. Such is the common interpretation of these lines and, given Dante's well-known sympathy for Can Grande, it appears the likely one. Another interpretation would have the "altered waters" refer to the malicious diversion of the Bacchiglione on the part of the Vicentini; "the folk" of line 48 could refer to either side. Perhaps this ambiguity is deliberate; Cunizza may well see this skirmish as merely another example of patricidal strife and contempt of imperial authority, with both sides at fault.[12]

From the misery of the many, Cunizza in her prophetic phase passes on to an individual tragedy. In Treviso (where the Sile and the Cagnano meet) there reigns now one Riccardo da Cammino (son of the "good Gherardo" of *Purgatorio* xvi, 124, son-in-law of Nino, "courteous judge" of *Purgatorio* viii, 53), for whom the "web" (*ragna*) is already being spread. Riccardo had become *signore* of Treviso only in 1306; when he was named imperial vicar his conversion to Ghibellinism did not meet with the approval of his subjects, and he was assassinated while playing chess (15 April 1312).[13] It would seem unlikely that the plot was already in the making in the year of the vision, but we cannot hold a sybil to arithmetical accuracy.

Woe to Padovani, Vicentini, and the Lord of Treviso! Woe also to Feltre, who will ere long have occasion to mourn the treachery (*difalta*) of her wicked bishop, Alessandro Novello, himself a Trevisano and so inevitably partaking of the ferocious nature of the *turba* aforementioned. In 1314 Alessandro handed over to Pino della Tosa, Angevin vicar of Ferrara, four political refugees of the Della Fontana families who had fled to him in expectation of sanctuary. Pino at once had them beheaded as rebels. Bad faith was always contemptible in the eyes of Dante; particularly shocking is such an act on the part of a priest: Cunizza does not hesitate to describe it as an act so "unseemly" that few criminals are incarcerated in Malta for worse deeds.[14] Malta for the ancient commentators was the clerical prison of Lake Bolsena; there were two other Maltas of the same nature, one in Viterbo, another in Padua. It seems to me that the passage gains in strength if we assume that Dante had no particular location in mind but was saying simply no criminal was ever incarcerated anywhere for a fouler crime.[15]

Cunizza lingers, as if fascinated, on the unholy conduct of this man of God: freely would this "obliging" (*cortese*) priest give buckets of (others') blood, not for the cause of the faith but to show himself a faithful Guelph. The association of *donerà* (will bestow), *cortese*, and *cotai doni* (such gifts), with their implications of feudal largesse, adds its own weight to the irony of the invective.

Noteworthy is the progression in the mounting scale of predicted horrors. First, warfare—common enough but stupid and perverse as seen from the vantage point of Paradise—then assassination, more shocking because more personal, and climactically treachery on the part of a man of God. Suiting the progression, reminiscent of the Infernal order, is the variation in Cunizza's tone as she surveys the successive crimes. The terzina (46–48) is cast in a definitely prophetic tone, solemn, distant, and as befits an oracle, slightly ambiguous. A certain obscurity is preserved in the prophecy touching Riccardo da Cammino. But her speech becomes much more personal and polemic in her denunciation of the Bishop of Feltre. To her as to her creator our poet, bad faith is the worst of sins, and we may assume that there is room in the ice of Antenora for the courteous cleric of Feltre, so willing to stop at nothing in order to *mostrarsi da parte* (show his partisanship). *Ex parte* indeed is Cunizza's entire invective; among the crimes she enumerates, two, the conspiracy and the betrayal, are acts of Guelphs; and one, the battle between Padovani and Vicentini, comes from a flouting (no matter how we interpret it) of imperial, which is to say Ghibelline, authority. At the end of her outburst comes a kind of ironic resignation. She concedes that the blood-stained generosity of the Bishop is not out of keeping with the "gifts" that are exchanged in "that part of the wicked land" and, almost as if recalling to herself her own station and half apologizing for her indignant speech, she closes, giving Dante her authority and her excuse:

> Mirrors there are above—you call them Thrones—
> From whence on us a judging God shines down,
> Making such words as mine seem good to us.
> (61–63)

It is appropriate that Cunizza's vision should come to her through the choir of Thrones; St. Thomas, following Gregory, had written *per tronum potestas judicaria designatur* (by throne the judicial power is indicated), and it is in their reflection that the privileged souls may behold the decision of Divine Justice. In the *Convivio* Dante had followed Brunetto Latini in associating this choir with Venus. In *Paradiso* xxviii, 125, he reveals that he has accepted the order established by Dionysius the Areopagite, by which Venus would come under the domination of Principalities. He has already indirectly made his correction in *Paradiso* viii, 34, where Charles Martel affirms: "We circle with the Celestial Princes." One suspects that he is here deliberately stressing the function of the choir of Thrones, having already made clear that it is no longer associated in his mind with this specific sphere.

So having spoken at length and with passion more earthly than saintly, yet revealing a noble if partisan concern for her kin and countrymen, Cunizza withdraws, forever to enjoy her eternal vision. As with the other saints, the rapid rotation of her enclosing illumination indicates her rapture.

> Here she fell silent, making evident
> Her thought was elsewhere, by the swift rotation
> To which she turned again even as before.
>
> (64–66)

It is now the turn of the "sparkling and precious gem," who, on Cunizza's departure, indicates by the intensity of his splendor that he too is eager to share his wisdom with Dante. The introduction of Folquet here has in its staging some resemblance to Guinizelli's presentation of Arnaut Daniel, the troubadour of the *Purgatorio*. Like Arnaut, Folquet has patiently bided his time, but on the departure of his sponsor steps forward without false modesty. As he waits for Dante's question he glows with the color of a ruby; love's color, be it Eros or Agape.

> The other jewel, already known to me
> As something dear, became before my eyes
> Like a rare ruby flashing in the sun.
>
> (67–69)

Still relatively new to Paradise, Dante cannot but remark on the ways of its citizens and, as Folquet glows before him, his memory goes back to other encounters in other worlds:

> Radiance up there is won through joyfulness
> As laughter here, while down below the shade
> Grows dark without, as sullen is the mind.
>
> (70–72)

So smiles of earth become the splendors of Paradise; but in the *Inferno*, where smiles of welcome are unknown, the reaction to an interlocutor is a darkening of the visage.[16] But Dante does not linger long on this reflection, for Folquet is waiting:

> "God sees all things and your sight so inHims
> Itself," said I, "O spirit blest, that no
> Desire may be evasive of your vision.
> Why then is not your voice, which gladdens Heaven,
> Blent with the song of those enraptured flames
> Who make themselves a cowl of their six wings—
> Why is it not responsive to my wish?
> I should not wait so long for your request
> If I could you me as you me yourself."
>
> (73–81)

Strange salutation indeed! The choice of words, the tortured structure, the esoteric image of line 78—are these indications that our poet too has fallen under the rhetorical influence of the star? Or are they an effort, involuntary perhaps, to match the ornate and stylized manner of the Provençal? For on every occasion that Dante has met a champion of the *langue d'oc* we have noted a suggestive linguistic obbligato: in the case of Arnaut Daniel he has allowed the poet to speak in his native tongue; the invective of *Purgatorio* vi, with its survey of inefficient rulers, echoes the *planh sirventes* of Sordello; and surely the scene of mangled bodies in *Inferno* xviii owes something to the *champs joncatz de quartiers* (field strewn with quarters) of Bertran de Born. And such is the richness of the troubadour's rhetoric here that all commentators paraphrase before glossing. My translation follows the conventional interpretation.

The passage abounds in unusual words. *Coculla* (cowl) appears nowhere else in the *Comedy* nor does *fuia* (evasive) anywhere else in the *Paradiso*, but the words that claim our principal attention are the new coined verbs: *inluiare* (inhim), *intuare* (inyou), *inmiare* (inme). These new coinages added to the *s'incinqua* (enfives) of line 40 give our canto a certain linguistic distinction. Such new and almost violently conceived creations well illustrate Dante's strategy in presenting the *Paradiso* not merely as the third of three realms or of three *cantiche* but as one by its very nature vastly different from the other two. This is the only *cantica* of which Dante says he does not know whether he sees the other world in the body or out of the body; it is the only realm where the "law of nature has no relevance." Earthly physics is superseded, and it is as natural to ascend in Heaven as it is to fall on earth. The reverse snowstorm (Canto xxvii, 67–69) and the backward-stated simile of ii, 22–24, reinforce the concept of a world totally different from ours. And in our mortal world we are indeed separate entities: *inluiare, intuare,* and *inmiare* are beyond our scope. But in Heaven, the terzina suggests, this is not so. But why again, we may ask ourselves, does Dante forge these new words, with their metaphysical implications, here and not elsewhere? Again because in Venus[17] we are in the domain of rhetoric? Rather, I think, because we are in the domain of love; the blending, the surrender, the infusion of one life into another, whether it be soul or body, is possible only through love; this is true no less mystically than biologically, and it is for this reason that the language of the mystic and the lover are the same. This Folquet, erstwhile lover and later saint, must know, and in a double sense Dante's new coined words must be part of Folquet's spiritual vocabulary.

Turning to the substance of 73–81, the reader cannot fail to be struck by the previously noted unparalleled insistence with which Dante seeks to learn the identity of the new *splendore*. It does suggest perhaps the eagerness of *Inferno* xxvi, 64–69, where, informed of the identity of the souls "within this flame," he presses Virgil for opportunity to speak with them. Can it be that here too he is aware of who is concealed within the new radiance of saintliness? Not impossible, but such a hypothesis is not necessary. Consider Dante's previous encounters in Paradise, in which after all at this point he is still quite new. On the moon, he discovers on his own account the presence of Piccarda, and after a gentle and somewhat general introduction by Beatrice he addresses her. On Mercury, he is still more interested in the reason for the souls' being where they are than in their individual identification, and in any case does not have to wait long for Justinian's self-revelation. In the case of Charles Martel, it is the soul who speaks first to Dante. Here for the first time the pilgrim's curiosity has been whetted: Cunizza has told him that he stands in the presence of a very famous man, whose name is destined to endure for centuries—and then has kept him waiting through a fairly lengthy discourse. His anticipation of meeting another soul of like stature to that of Justinian (or perhaps one whose presence may be as puzzling as Cunizza's to the *vulgo*?) must be keen indeed. Hence his impatience is very natural, though its expression verges, as we have seen, on the discourteous.

Like Cunizza, Folquet begins by indicating the region of his birth but with a much more ample periphrasis, which, for all its geographical information, does not seem entirely convincing poetically. Is Folquet here (as Pietrobono suspects) reproaching Dante for the impatience we have noted? Whatever the motive may have been for Dante's impatience Folquet

seems to consider it unbecoming; hence his leisurely reply, full
of irrelevant erudition:

> "The vastest valley in which water spreads"
> Such the beginning of his words to me,
> "Save for that sea engarlanding the earth,
> Extends so far between discordant strands
> Against the sun, that its meridian
> It makes of what was its horizon first."
>
> (82–87)

First a description of the Mediterranean, largest of seas except for mighty Ocean, which embraces the earth, extending
from West to East (from Gibraltar to Jerusalem), a full
ninety degrees of the earth's circumference—such is the sense
of lines 86–87. Dante in thus enlarging the Mediterranean (it
covers actually only forty-two degrees) was simply accepting
the scientific theory of his time.[18] We may see, incidentally, in
the discordant shores something more than an echo of the Virgilian *litora litoribus contraria*: Dante probably is thinking of
the Mediterranean as a division between the Christian and Mo-
hammedan worlds. Folquet, continuing, narrows somewhat
his range finders:

> I was a dweller on that valley's shore
> Flanked by the Ebro and the Macra, which,
> Though short, parts Genoa from Tuscany.
> Alike almost for sunset and for dawn
> Bougia lies and the town from whence I sprung,
> That warmed of old its harbor with its blood.
>
> (88–93)

He sprang then from the region on the northern shore of
the Mediterranean basin, which is bounded by the Macra
(which for a portion of its course serves as a boundary between Tuscany and Liguria) and the Ebro in Spain, a region

large enough to leave Dante still not much wiser. As if taking pity on him, Folquet, with some acceleration of rhythm, reveals (though still periphrastically) the city of his birth; it is directly across the Mediterranean from Bougia (as Dante, still faithful to the only charts he knew, thought it was) and, lest there be any doubt, it was the city that had once made the waters of its harbor red with its own blood. All this in place of saying Marseilles! The critics have seen in this pompous style an echo of troubadour subtlety, but I wonder if the last line, with its echo of *Pharsalia* III, 571, describing the blood-flecked harbor of Marseilles on the occasion of Caesar's victory over Pompey's forces, may not afford us another clue. For Dante's much-admired Lucan would have provided him with exactly the kind of turgid rhetoric which characterizes this passage.

Perhaps the lengthy preface serves a certain moral purpose: four terzinas to a description of the speaker's birthplace; less than two lines for a disclosure, framed in terms almost excessively humble, of his name.

> Folco they called me, those to whom my name
> Was known, and this encircling sphere is stamped
> By me as once I was impressed by it.
>
> (94–97)

A modest disclaimer of Cunizza's compliment, and Folquet does not linger on the things for which his fame will endure. Like Cunizza again, his first thought is to confess his human weakness. Cunizza "indulges herself"; Folquet seems to reveal a certain satisfaction at the strength of his carnal passions.

> For Belus' daughter no more hotly burned
> Offensive to Sichaeus and Creüsa,
> Than I, while it accorded to my locks;
> Nay, nor the Rhodopean maid, deceived
> By Demophoön, nor Alcides himself
> When he took Iole into his heart.
>
> (97–102)

One cannot escape the conviction that what is displayed before us in these lines of classical reminiscence is not so much the *via amoris* of Folquet as the erudition of Dante Alighieri. Folquet would have us believe that his love of his lady—or possibly ladies—had the exaggerated madness of the passions of a Dido or a Phyllis, both suicides, and the infatuated abasement of Hercules for the girl Iole. This is to claim much, and insofar as the words are in character at all they bespeak a pride in sin somewhat out of place in a saint. Nor in fact does Folquet do justice to himself; there is nothing in his life or his works to suggest quite the degree of passion which he hints at here, even though Zingarelli points out the verb *arse* (burned) is a linguistic echo of some of Folquet's *cansos*.[19]

Folquet was born in Marseilles, son of a Genoese merchant, who left him a considerable substance.[20] His Provençal biographer tells of his faithful and unrequited love for the wife of Lord Barral and how, on the death of his lady and his patrons he "abandoned the world." It is a story of devotion, but it has none of the sensuality of William of Poitou, the amorous obsession of Bernart de Ventadorn or the erotic madness of Peire Vidal. Folquet's surviving verses support the impression we get from the biography; they reveal an intellectual and a technician, in love as much with his own rhetoric as with his lady; a kind of embryonic Petrarch (and Messer Francesco does indeed speak well of him), but hardly passion's slave. Folquet is remembered not for his erotic excess but for his conversion (or apostasy); he abandoned not so much the world as the *gai saber*, for he did not end his days in a monastery but as Bishop of Toulouse (appointed in 1205), an active and prominent participant in the Albigensian Crusade, which demolished the chivalrous society wherein as a youth he had played a part. He died in 1231. His rôle in the extirpation of heresy is mentioned with approval, as might be expected, in the *Speculum morale* of Vincent of Beauvais and the *De triumphiis ecclesiae libri octo* of Johannes de Garlandia; less flattering is the appellation given him in the *Chanson de la Croisade*, where Count Ray-

mond of Foix, speaking in the presence of the Pope, says of
him that he seems rather the Anti-Christ than a legate of
Rome.

If Folquet's desire to make a dogmatic point leads him to
exaggerate the strength of his erotic impulse, yet in the conventional sense he had been, as were all the troubadours, a
lover, and among lovers his conversion makes him the most
likely choice for election to Dante's Paradise. Nor would the
Paradiso have been complete without a troubadour; the symmetry of Dante's plan calls for a representative of that tradition. Yet there are other reasons too for Dante's admiration.
Our poet saw in Folquet a great stylist; he quotes him with approval in *De vulgari eloquentia* II, vi, 6, and he probably took
from him the allusion to the multiplication of the chess board
in *Paradiso* XXVIII, 93. And the polished style, full of antitheses
and sententious phrases, was sure to appeal to one who found
so much to admire in Arnaut Daniel. Further, though Folquet
was a poet and lover, he was a Crusader too; a poet who was
also a lover, an intellectual, and a champion of the faith could
hardly fail of a place in Dante's hierarchy. It may well be too
that Dante saw some resemblance between his own experiences
and those of Folquet; our poet had also written verses of love
(unrequited and Platonic) in his youth, and with the death of
the beloved had embarked on a new life. As we have remarked
in an essay above, Folquet has had a bad name among moderns:
Stroński does well to point out that it is due in large part to a
willful distortion of the material in the *Chanson de la Croisade*
by the anonymous fifteenth-century author of the prose version. Dante, like his contemporaries, would have seen him as
Stroński describes him, in words we quoted earlier—"A man
of superior intelligence and prodigious activity"—and a good
man as well, for tales of his kindness are not wanting.

As a figure in the *Paradiso* Folquet serves, as Cunizza
served, to unify the poem by evocation of other figures on the
long journey. Not only does he cast our memory back to Arnaut Daniel and Bertran de Born, but his reference to Dido in

line 97 carries us back to the less fortunate lovers of *Inferno* v, also burning in an eternal fire. So again, less obtrusively than in the case of Cunizza, the contrasting destinies of these servants of love are brought to our attention.

Having described his passion with classical references, which he must have learned since coming to Heaven, since nothing of that nature is to be found in his verses, Folquet goes on to rephrase the dogmatic law, already stated more economically, if less expertly, by Cunizza:

> Yet here there's no repentance, nay, we smile,
> Not for the fault, which comes not to our minds,
> But for the Power that ordained and foresaw.
> Here we look closely on the art adorning
> Such great effect, and mark the good whereby
> The world above governs the one below.
>
> (103–108)

The explicit nature of Folquet's speech here calls forth a question that might also have been asked of Cunizza: how can the troubadour bishop say that his sin *non torna a mente*, when as a matter of fact he shows in the preceding terzinas that he recalls it perfectly? It is Buti who reminds us that Lethe does not erase the memory of the act but only of the evil impulse that occasioned it; *la colpa* (the fault), says Scartazzini, *non torna a mente come colpa* (is not remembered as a fault).[21] The smile of the blessed, not devoid of complacency, springs from the consideration of the divine art (*valor*), whose providence had ordained that—at least in certain cases —such influences as that of Venus could lead to salvation. So, like Cunizza, but in language more precise and more classical (and for that reason less humanly appealing), Folquet too *lietamente s'indulge*.

Terzina 106–108, a continuation of and a gloss on 103–105, presents its own puzzle. In my English version I have followed Sapegno's interpretation, which goes back ultimately to Lana and the *Ottimo*. It is certainly not Dante's happiest terzina from the point of view of clarity, and if the repetition of *torna* (appearing in rhyme in 104 and 108) be a gesture toward the ambiguous rhyming of the Provençals, it may be said that Dante's Folquet, unlike the historical one, shows an unhappy devotion to the *trobar clus*, or obscure style.

Perhaps divining that Dante has had enough of this ornate speech or possibly feeling that he has spoken sufficiently of himself, Folquet prepares to focus the heavenly pilgrim's attention on the third figure of this canto—the fourth if we include Charles Martel, as we may.

> But now, that you may bear away fulfilled
> Every desire this sphere has roused in you,
> Yet further it behooves me to proceed.
> You wish to know who is within this light
> Standing beside me and as scintillant
> As a sunbeam in a pellucid pool.
>
> (109–114)

Has Dante, one wonders, given any sign of impatience? Inwardly he must have revealed his eagerness to know the identity of Folquet's neighbor. Here Folquet's speech is clear and indeed colorless save for line 114, the only truly paradisiacal line in our canto. Two pure elements, the sunshine and the "pellucid" (*mera*) water, suggest perfectly the limpid and simple happiness of a soul purified and sanctified; the latter element recalls to the reader's subconscious other uses of water as parallels to the encompassing and cleansing atmosphere of Paradise; in fact it echoes, though with less scientific verbiage, Dante's figure for his own reception into the first heavenly sphere (*Par.* II, 35–36).

> Learn that therein in all tranquility
> Dwells Rahab, who, joined to our order, gave
> Her impress to it with the deepest stamp.
> By this heaven, where the shadow of your world
> Reaches its point, she was assumed before

> All other souls who rose with Christ triumphant.
>
> (115–120)

The same simple beauty carries over into line 115; the verb is particularly appropriate, being active and reflexive, yet expressing a condition of happy acceptance (greater, perhaps, because freer of the political context, than that of Cunizza).

Lines 118–119 remind us that we are coming to the close of the first great division of the *Paradiso*. Dante, basing his conviction on the Arabian astronomer, Alfraganus,[22] puts into the mouth of Folquet a scientific statement: the long, cone-like shadow of the earth, which we may assume to have enveloped the moon and Mercury, comes to its point on Venus. Scientific truth here hardly veils the allegory. Up to now we have seen souls whose aspiration or absolute will, to use the language of Beatrice, has secured their salvation but who, with imperfectly conditioned wills, have yet retained something of the earthly. Active in the service of God, they have fought the good fight as well as they could and have received their crown. But all—through inconstancy, vainglory, or impurity—have yielded somewhat to the attractions or the pressures of mortality. The three successive circles will present to us souls of higher endowment, though with attributes that in a sense parallel those of the first three heavens—and Dante's introduction to Canto x will make the distinction clear. Here that glorious preface is hinted at in Folquet's matter-of-fact comment. It is appropriate that the reminder should come at this time; it serves almost as a punctuation mark; and it is appropriate too that it should be assigned to the erudite Bishop of Toulouse.

Of Rahab, Folquet uses the same figure that he has used of himself; as he imprints himself upon the heaven of Venus, so is she stamped thereon; her imprint is deeper, not because her sin was greater, although that argument could be defended, but because of her prominence in history and ecclesiastical allegory. As in the series of anagogical *rapprochements*, Joshua, Samson, and even Adam were seen as figures of Christ, so

Rahab was considered a figure of the Church.[23] Zingarelli finds it fitting that Folquet, who aided in the triumph of the Crusaders over heresy, should introduce the figure who played a parallel role in a similar victory in the Old Testament;[24] Rahab had protected the spies sent by Joshua into Jericho (Joshua II, 1–24; VI, 17–25; Hebrews XI, 31, and James II, 25). Her brave act is related by Folquet, whose virtuosity in rich rhymes once more finds expression:

> And right it was to leave her in some heaven
> To be a palm of that high victory
> Which was achieved by one palm and the other,
> For she it was who comforted the first
> Glory of Joshua in the Holy Land
> (Which hardly touches the Pope's memory).
>
> (121–126)

Most modern commentators follow Benvenuto in seeing in line 123 an allusion to the wounds made by the nails in Christ's hand (*quia intraque manu fuit affixus cruci*) rather than to Joshua's conquest of Jericho by prayer (*tollendo manus suas*, Ecclesiasticus XLVI, 3), and this interpretation seems preferable; not only would the *alta vittoria* (high victory) then have the noble and eternal sense of the triumph of the Church, but the parallel Joshua-Rahab and Christ and the Church would be clearly if subtly affirmed. Truly the prefiguration of such a triumph should find its place "in a certain heaven." [25]

Line 126 brings us with a shock out of the language of figures and out of the high austerity of the Old Testament into the modern world of cold facts and cynical prelates. It is again Dante's old enemy who is here under attack; Benvenuto does well to recall *Inferno* XXVII, 85–89. Yet nothing is to prevent us from believing that Dante may have had in mind the Pope *regnant* at the time these lines were written, for in the view of Cacciaguida's descendant all the Popes of his day were negligent of their primary duty.

We have said that Rahab is not and cannot be concerned

with the politics of the fourteenth century. From her lips come no word and certainly no invective. Yet to balance the veiled prophecy of Charles Martel and the more specific predictions of Cunizza, the figure of Rahab too has its political and apocalyptic appendage—only it is, as it were, spoken for her by Folquet. Thus her majestic aloofness is preserved while the polemic aspect which, in Dante's intention, each of the figures in Venus should present is not overlooked. And as Charles has, though gently, taken to task the House of Naples, and Cunizza has excoriated the Guelph faction, Folquet—or is it Rahab who inspires him?—turns his crusading sword against the venality of the papacy and the ultimate source of that venality, the avaricious villa by the Arno:

> Your city, which is the plant of that same being
> Who first upon his Maker turned his back,
> And whose envy is so bitterly lamented
> Produces and sends forth the accursed flower
> Which has misled the sheep and tender lambs,
> For it has changed their shepherd into wolf.
>
> (127–132)

We may notice the ornamental appropriateness of the juxtaposition of *pianta* (plant) and *fiore* (flower), though the effect is more rhetorical than poetic; we may observe yet another *rime riche* (the fourth in this canto) falling from the lips of our rhetorical troubadour: yet such details will not distract us from the intensity of Dante's speech, never more firm or clear than when he is aiming at his beloved and hated Florence. The reference to Lucifer's foundation of Florence we may take as a moral observation or more likely see in it an association of the pagan deity Mars, Florence's first patron (*Inf.* XIII, 144 *sq.*), with a devil, a servant of Satan if not the Prince of Darkness himself. Such was the view taken of the pagan gods by the Church Fathers. But now comes the turn of the second party in the iniquitous alliance of avarice. The Church too has been perverted by the lust for gain.

> Because of this the Gospel and the great
> Doctors are put aside; now the Decretals
> Alone are studied, as their margins show.
>
> (133–135)

On these lines d'Ovidio quotes the comment of Pietro Damiano which Dante seems to echo: "The Gospels are left unread . . . the priests' lips are opened only to argue legal cases." [26] Naturally the Decretals (here in the sense of the corpus of Canon Law) would show their hard usage by the worn condition of their margins. No doubt a common charge, but we may admire the vigor of the terzina and the realistic detail of its last line. Folquet has put aside his elaborate style and speaks out like an honest Christian—like Dante Alighieri, indeed. And he rounds off his invective with another reference to the Holy Land, this time suggestive of the charity (as the former had been of the zeal) that should inspire the corrupt curia, intent on "the accursed flower" (*il maledetto fiore*, the "this" of line 136) at the cost of their proper duties.

> This is the Pope's and Cardinals' concern
> And their thoughts never turn to Nazareth
> Where Gabriel unfolded once his wings.
>
> (136–138)

And Folquet concludes, as Charles Martel and Cunizza have concluded, with a prophecy of God's vengeance, here specifically aimed at the *Roma falsa e tafura* (false and treacherous Rome—to use a phrase from one of Folquet's compatriots[27]— which is, even more than Florence, the center of the world's iniquity, as it should be of its virtue. And it is a priest who speaks.

> But soon
> The Vatican and the other chosen parts
> Of Rome which have become the cemetery
> For the true soldiery that followed Peter
> Will be delivered from the adulterous yoke.
>
> (137–142)

Adultero echoes the *avolterate* of *Inferno* xix, and in fact the passages are of the same substance. The prophecy here has been variously interpreted as referring to the death of Boniface VIII, the transfer of the papal see to Avignon, or the coming of Henry VII. More likely it is simply, as are other prophecies of similar nature in this canto and elsewhere, an expression of Dante's faith in the savior Veltro, who will come in God's own time to restore justice to the world.

On this note of prophetic exaltation our canto ends. It is a canto which reveals Dante's preoccupation with the events of his time, a canto which has in it very little that is truly paradisiacal and even less of the metaphysical. It displays, however, better than most, Dante's virtuosity as well as his moral rectitude. It is a canto that must be considered not on its own but in close connection with Canto viii. If we so consider it, and review Dante's exploration of the star last touched by the earth's shadow, we shall find the characters chosen to exemplify its effects just what we might expect: warm-hearted, devoted souls whose interest in their fellowman may take a didactic or a polemic twist but is always sincere, overt, and, save for Rahab, articulate. There are four champions, two of each sex as becomes the law of Venus, all of whom have had political as well as amatory experience. The passion that inflamed them and, once refined, exalted them was never that of selfish lust, and whatever else one may say of them they lived for others. Their concern now, if it be earth-directed, is also love-motivated. Vossler[28] reminds us that "the three upper planetary heavens repeat the motifs of the three lower ones." And when we reach the sphere of Jupiter we shall find not merely illustrations but champions of the God-inspired human search for justice, having learned in this canto that it is inseparable from love. David, Trajan, and Constantine await us here too as earth-transcendent figures. But let us observe that here in earth-darkened Venus, in the sphere of *principi celesti*, earthly princes also speak. One is a secular ruler, another a great lady, a third prince of the Church. Loftier by far will

be the language heard in Jupiter, but here too the language of
the souls whom Dante meets—and the poet's likewise while he
is with them—has its own distinction; we are not likely to forget that we are in the heaven associated with rhetoric, "sweet-
est of all sciences."

8
Light from Mars

ह∾

I don't think any study basing itself on the rôle and significance of Cacciaguida needs any particular apology. Sapegno
remarks that "the vastness of design of the Martian chapter is
rivaled only by the great encounter with Beatrice in the ter-
restial paradise," and for Carlo Steiner the Cacciaguida cantos
are simply "the most solemn episode of the *Comedy*." [1] One
might, of course, object that quite enough has been said about
the central figure. No reader of the *Comedy* can fail to be
impressed by his dignity and vigor, which seem to make the
rest of Heaven's gallery look a little pale by comparison. Perhaps in a sense he doesn't belong in Heaven—of that we may
say more later. My only apology for this excursion on tolerably familiar ground is that the studies of Mars and its most
articulate inhabitant have suffered a little from the fragmenta-
tion which follows inevitably on the size of the episode and
the traditional modes of Dante study. The commentators,
from whom I shall cheerfully rob a fair proportion of what I
have to say, annotate line by line; the authors of the sundry
Lecturae Dantis limit themselves to one canto. I should like
here to survey the whole chapter as a unit and comment on
such facets of the old Crusader as appeal to me and for which I
can find room. He deserves not merely a chapter but a book.
And if I call my remarks "Light from Mars" it is because it is

in Mars that our poet gets his ultimate illumination concerning his mission, and we, his readers, not only share in this kind of illumination but get a little dividend of our own in following tangential reflections which emanate from this *vivo topazio,* this handsomely set jewel from the author's workshop. I shall add only that if my subject seems at first sight a little specialized I think that following these tangents will show us that this is not so. There are moments when the whole *Comedy* comes into focus—when, in capsule form, it is, as it were, all there. One such moment surely is in Canto 1 of the *Inferno,* although you have to read the poem to be aware of it. Another, perhaps, occurs against the background of the earthly Paradise. But I am inclined to think that as a kind of tissue sample the Cacciaguida episode is the richest of all we could select. Umberto Cosmo[2] found it not only the heart of the *Comedy* but also the ultimate crucible of themes and attitudes apparent in the minor works, from the *Canzoni* to the *Epistolae.*

We have remarked, in the essay on *Paradiso* IX, on the artistry with which Dante mingles his various measures of time and structure. There is the regular metronomic beat of the canto; against this the measures of his physical divisions of circles, terraces, and spheres; and interwoven with these are the thematic allotments, as it were. The interplay of these various measures is for me a constant delight. I think, although it is not my purpose to develop the point here, that the poet grows more skillful at this kind of manipulation, and perhaps indeed even more aware of its possibilities, as the poem moves on. As touching the *Paradiso,* I think it may be said that the canto measure is much more regular than in the other *cantiche*— none of the cantos of the *Paradiso* is either unusually long or unusually short, and two thirds of them are of almost identical length. To which may be added also that the physical divisions are more spacious than in the other *cantiche;* there are many subdivisions in Hell, and in the case of Purgatory the allotment of a somewhat disproportionate space to both ante-Purgatory and the terrestrial paradise allows the terraces themselves only eighteen cantos. But in the *Paradiso* there is no ante-Heaven and no afterpiece corresponding to the terrestrial paradise. The spheres are wide and roomy as they ought to be. Given more space and a somewhat smaller cast of characters— this too, however deplorable, is only to be expected—than we have in the other two kingdoms, it is only natural that conversations should be longer and more leisurely and that the kind of homily, so objectionable to Croce, should flourish.

Even so the allotment given Cacciaguida calls for special notice. His domain comprises three full cantos and parts of two others, a total of 550 lines, a larger span than that given to any other character in the *Comedy*, save for the major guides Virgil and Beatrice. Add to this that the position of Cacciaguida is highly strategic, covering the central cantos of the *Paradiso* and placed in the central heaven, and the poet's intention becomes even clearer. Cacciaguida is meant to be the central figure of the crowning *cantica*. What he has to say is important; what he subsumes, prefigures, and symbolizes more important still.

Let us begin with a word about his habitat. Dante did not come to Mars as a tourist unprepared for his journey; he had read his guide-books and indeed written one of his own about such extra-terrestrial excursions. In the second tractate of the *Convivio* he speaks in some detail of Mars; he reminds us that it is the fifth of the moving heavens and hence occupies the central position, which Dante describes as in a "harmonious relationship" to the other spheres. This suggests that in the Table of Sciences matching the heavens, music, also a study of harmonies, may be associated with this planet. Dante adds that its power of drying and burning things also gives it properties akin to music, which can draw off the vapors from the heart. He tells us too that these enclosing vapors as they burn may signify the death of kings, recalling that Seneca saw aloft a globe of fire at the time of the death of Augustus and that many of these vapors attached to Mars were seen aflame in the form of the Cross in Florence at the time of its ruin (meaning, in the opinion of most critics, at the time of the entrance of Charles of Valois into the city). The celestial officials assigned to Mars are those of the second order of the second hierarchy, the Virtues whose office it is to contemplate the Son with reference to his own person. Perhaps the repetition of *Cristo* in rhyme is meant to suggest this function to us. I believe all of these preliminary notes find their way unobtrusively into the definitive version of Mars as we now enter it. But the first thing we notice is that it is red; *affocato* (fiery) and *roggio* (ruddy) are the immediate terms of reference. This too the *Convivio* had prepared us for; it is interesting that the word *affocato* appears in both the *Convivio* and the *Paradiso* as descriptive of the planet.

This first sense impression of a visual nature is followed by a similar auditive impression, again, I believe, unique in the *Comedy*. For Dante hears arise from the myriad saintly voices of the inhabitants of this heaven a song, audible but not comprehensible, as one might hear harmonious notes of a viol and a harp without quite following the melodic line. This is the first substantial musical figure of the *Paradiso*, and its placing here is surely meant to remind us of the affinity that this planet has with music, even as the *Convivio* affirmed. As for the hymn sung, Dante can make out only the words, "Arise and conquer," which can be applied to Christ, whose symbol dominates this heaven, to the Crusader who died for it, and to Dante's own mission, which will require his arising from his contingent misfortunes to conquer both as poet and prophet.

For purposes of closer study we may divide the Cacciaguida episode into four quite well defined sections. The first, which might be called "Preparation and Salutation," runs from Canto xiv, line 85 (where Dante becomes aware of his rising to Mars), to Canto xv, line 97, a total of 151 lines. The second part—the Old Florence motif—begins almost without warning, immediately after Cacciaguida completes his self-introduction (xv, 97), and, with necessary interruptions for the sake of drama and dialectic, runs right on through Canto xvi, a total of 206 lines. The third part, which we could call "Prediction and Prescription," is essentially Canto XVII, although a kind of lingering aftertaste may be said to carry us through line 6 of Canto XVIII, a total of 148 lines. The last part, after a brief transitional passage, presents a rather impersonal Cacciaguida, who points out his distinguished companions with the curator-like air of any other of Dante's numerous instructors over the course of his journey; this is the section of the official, not to say officious, Cacciaguida and is on most counts the least interesting of the Martian sections.

The first three divisions are, however, not merely interesting and significant but I should say uniquely valuable for the understanding of the poem and the poet. To begin with the actual encounter, dramatic in its own right and rich in associations both in the framework of the *Comedy* itself and in Dante's cultural preparation, Cacciaguida's first outburst—it is the appropriate word—is in Latin. But Dante does not entirely take it in, particularly as it is followed by even loftier and hence quite unintelligible discourse. The first words Dante really understands make up lines 47 and 48: "Blessed be thou, trine and one, who art so courteous toward my seed." Here is delight, gratitude to God, and, although it may not be entirely justified, what seems very much like an element of surprise. These emotional ingredients have been found in two of Dante's previous encounters—and only two. In the burning desert of the violent, Dante had heard a voice, crying out with much the same mixture of emotions *Qual meraviglia* (what a marvel), and among the penitent gluttons there was one who could echo the same remark (in more Christian language): *Qual grazia m'è questa* (What grace is this to me). Of these Brunetto and Forese are not the only souls who recognize Dante before he recognizes them (we recall Ciacco as another, and Casella and Belacqua; most of them are Florentines, we may note), but they are the only ones who do so with excited and affectionate eagerness. And, perhaps more to the point, intimacy. It is interesting to note that both stress the marvelous and exceptional nature of the encounter, as climactically as Cacciaguida does here. The Lingering on this truth we become aware of Cacciaguida's function—or rather two of his functions—in the *Comedy:* he is at once the crown and climax of the Florentine motif and the confirmation of the miraculous nature of Dante's journey.

Of all the characters in the poem Cacciaguida is the only one to greet the pilgrim in Latin. The closest parallel to its use here is the passage describing the advent of Beatrice in the *Purgatorio,* where Latin appears in three rhyming lines. But even this is not quite the same. Cacciaguida is given this distinction in order to acquire more dignity in the eyes of the reader and to remind us linguistically of the association between Dante and Aeneas. This connection is clearly pointed out by lines 25–27 of Canto xv.

> Even so Anchises' pious shade came forth,
> If we may give credence to our greatest muse,
> When in Elysium he beheld his son.

I do not think we need be troubled by Curtius' statement that the encounter is inspired by the *Dream of Scipio* and that Dante is again "concealing his sources." [3] The association the poet wants to make is not with Scipio but with Aeneas. Far from concealing his sources he is practically giving us a footnote. And in fact we have been prepared for this ever since Canto II of the *Inferno,* where the poet's denial, *Io non Enea io non Paolo sono* (Aeneas am I not, nor am I Paul) was really an affirmation. Lest we should forget, the Virgilian *sanguis meus* is another sign; and evidence of further identification with the heroic wanderer of the classical past may be seen in the interweaving of Latin rhymes in an Italian fabric; this is the only time, I think, that Dante composes verses in Latin truly integrated with the rhyme scheme of his native Tuscan.

Linguistic matters in truth loom large in the introductory

section of the episode. First the Latin, then the language incomprehensible to Dante—I think the implication is that it was not Latin, but purely celestial—and finally the ecstatic expression of gratitude and the partial identification in the phrase *nel mio seme*, which has to be glossed later on for the astonished Dante: *io fui la tua radice* (I was your root). The happy excitement of the encounter is reinforced by the nature of the communication; such rapture must of necessity wait a while for its proper and adequate expression.

Not everyone has been satisfied with the implications of Aeneas here. Perhaps the case for another allusion is put best and most recently by Professor Mazzeo. Beginning with a reference to the line of *Inferno* II I quoted above, he goes on: "Dante very subtly takes up the Aeneas-Paul parallel again in *Paradiso* xv when he meets his ancestor Cacciaguida, a gem in the cross of souls in the heaven of Mars, who leaves it to come to greet Dante. Cacciaguida then exclaims in Latin: 'O my own blood! O grace of God poured forth above measure! To whom as to thee was heaven's gate ever opened twice?'

"The answer is obvious," continues Professor Mazzeo, "even though Dante does not give it. Such an experience was given to St. Paul. If Cacciaguida is, in Dante's private typology, an Anchises, then Dante is an Aeneas, but a celestial and Christian Aeneas, for the pagan real Aeneas is in limbo (*Inf.* IV, 122). The truly archetypal Christian Aeneas—again in Dante's private typology—is St. Paul. He is the Christian parallel, and to him if to anyone, were the gates of heaven open twice, rapt while in this life to the highest heaven. What Dante here seems to be saying is that St. Paul received a unique vision shared by no other—except Dante himself." [4]

More daring still and remarkable for being a little ahead of its time is the theory advanced more than thirty years ago by H. F. Dunbar, who sees Dante as a Christ figure and nowhere more clearly so than in the Cacciaguida episode. Practically all commentators have picked up the scriptural echo in xv, 88,

"O leaf of mine, in whom I was well pleased," and some have remembered its adumbration in *Inferno* VIII, "Blessed be she who bore thee," but Miss Dunbar developed the suggestion. It will be convenient here to summarize her arguments even though it will take us beyond the section we are now dealing with. Assuming, on the basis of the letter to Can Grande, that we must apply to the *Comedy* the same rules of interpretation that we employ for scripture and asserting that Dante conceived of his office as a philosophical guide to the vicar of the Emperor, she then continues: "In the simile comparing the welcome of Dante by Cacciaguida to that of Aeneas by Anchises is a reminiscence of that aspect of Dante's personal life in which his function was akin to that of Aeneas, preparation for the human mission of Christ. There would seem to be at the same time a suggestion of an equation of Cacciaguida to David, from whose blood Christ sprang. The allegorical burden is more clearly defined in Cacciaguida's greeting: '*O superinfusa*' and in his rhetorical question '*sicut tibi, cui bis unquam coeli ianua reclusa*,' which implies the answer, 'Christ.' "

She adds further arguments related to her thesis as follows: "The reference to the Lion in Canto XVI is to Christ as the Lion of the tribe of Judah; Mars is the sphere in which Dante sees the cross. In Mars, for the first time, the central attention of the poem is directed toward Christ, Christ in his human earthly life. Like the Milky Way, dotted with various-sized points of light, so in the heart of the Mars 'those rays disposed/ In constellations formed the sacred sign/ which quadrants jointed within the round portray.' The signification of this earthly life of Christ was the Cross, with its song of victory so far above mortal perception that neither the agony nor the triumph could be reached by human imagination.

> So from the lights that gleamed before me there
> Along the cross a melody arose
> Which ravished me though I seized not the song.

All of the sweet song that could be grasped by the understanding was its refrain: 'Rise thou up and conquer' in the strength of Christ who has won the victory."

"Dante is in three respects a type of Christ," she continues, "so far as this story is concerned: first, as above, in his typical human nature; second, in his destined and foretold sufferings, which Dante, having had previous forebodings and partial prophecies, sees here in the light of eternity."

"Third, in the fruits of his victory also, Dante is a type of Christ as shown by the answer to his query as to whether, under the foreseen conditions, he is to tell the whole truth." [5]

The mission, then, that is to be spelled out by Cacciaguida later on is hinted at by the symbolic language of the salutation and Dante's accompanying commentary. And if he is at once a new Aeneas and a Christ-figure this is only as it should be for a poet and prophet who is to serve both Church and State.

What may be called the Florentine stream, which makes up a large proportion of Cacciaguida's homily, is fascinating in its implications. In part it is evocative and nostalgic, in part rather arid chronicle. What shall we make of the picture of old Florence with its sober manners, its tranquil way of life, its solid virtues, Victorian, one might say, *avant la lettre?* I confess that I find the loving depiction of this lost world of happiness and propriety rather odd on the lips of a saint in Paradise. He seems to be recalling *la vita serena* with all the wistful nostalgia of a soul in the *Inferno*. We all but have the feeling that he was happier in Florence than he is in Heaven. The irreverent thought crosses our mind that had he not had the good fortune to perish fighting the infidel and so be assured of his celestial passport we might well have found him in one of the lower realms. Unlike Piccarda, who discourses on the nature of Heaven, or Charles Martel, who has something to say of the education of princes, indeed even unlike Cunizza, who knows that Italy is a "wicked land" and is glad to be out of it, Cacciaguida's heart is still filled with the concerns of his earthly home. We sense that, if the Florence of 1300 were at all like that of 1148, he would be only too happy to return. I may add too that I find a somewhat disconcerting complacency which I do not normally associate with sanctity in his line, *insieme fui cristiano e Cacciaguida* (at once/ A Christian I became and Cacciaguida); the name put in the position of the metrical emphasis, the line echoing, or so it seems to me, *Cesare fui e son Giustiniano* (Caesar was I and am Justinian).

The tone here, that of melancholy longing for a lost world of innocence, is matched only by that which accompanies the description of the earthly Paradise in the last cantos of the *Purgatorio*. In fact one might almost say that this is the lost paradise of history, as Eden is the lost paradise of myth. Momigliano remarks of this passage that the Florence of Cacciaguida's memory seems to have been indeed an anticipation of Heaven itself. It is secular enough in all truth; the virtues extolled by Dante's sainted ancestor are the old virtues of sobriety, chastity, moderation, centered as much on the conduct of womankind as on anything else, recalling the example of the Roman matrons voiced by the gluttonous on the sixth terrace of the mount. It is noteworthy that the examples of the virtuous chosen to contrast with the present dissolute characters of Dante's Florence are classical figures, such as Cincinnatus and Cornelia, rather than Christian models, and the fairy tales that mothers told their children were based on classical stories of Troy and Fiesole and Rome, with no mention either of the Old Testament or the lives of the saints. Dino Provenzal points out more clearly than most that the great Christian lesson is there to be learned: Florence was a perfect community but it decayed; the women were once modest but nowadays they are dedicated to ostentation and luxury; Cacciaguida followed the Emperor, but to death and not triumph; the Crusades themselves have failed. From all of which we may draw the same lesson that Beatrice hammered home to our penitent wayfarer on the top of the mountain: earthly things, *le presenti cose*, however fair, are transient and will either pass away or decay; only the things of the spirit abide with us forever.

Sapegno makes the same point. And of course it is a sound one; still I confess to a certain sympathy with the old romantic interpretation. Granted earthly things must pass—still affectionate memory can see them as beautiful in their very fragility. And what Dante is telling us here (as interpreted by Provenzal, Sapegno, and company) is not quite what Cacciaguida is saying. For the rest I shall not linger on the vexed lines that occur in the course of this wistful evocation. Many commentators have fought out the battle as to which *cerchia antica* the poet had in mind, whether it was *donne contigiate* (fine-shod ladies) or elaborate gowns, and whether or not Cacciaguida knew which Emperor he was talking about. I shan't worry those old bones any further here. I will say, with regard to the remark in line 120 that in the good old days no Florentine wife was left deserted in bed "because of France," as nowadays (1300), that the suggestion of Donadoni[6] pleases me. Most commentators see in this a reference to the increasing traffic with France on the part of Florentine merchants. Donadoni however puts the line in context with the first line of the terzina, in which it is said that the women were sure of their place of burial (that is, did not follow their husbands into exile and so die far from home) and believes that desertion "because of France" refers to the intervention of Charles of Valois and the consequent exile of many leaders of the Whites. This can then be connected with Cacciaguida's memorable description of the arrows of exile in Canto XVII: "You will abandon everything you love/ most dearly"—first of all among them, we should hope, Gemma. One cannot strictly say that Dante was speaking of himself, but we do know that Gemma did not accompany him.

The Florentine stream, if I may preserve the figure, while continuing to run strong and clear as we move into Canto XVI, one of the three longest cantos of the *Paradiso*, shifts into direction a little, from the idyllic and semi-mythical to the statistical. Dream yields to chronicle as Cacciaguida, carried away by reminiscence, cannot refrain from citing all the great families

of the past, much as an old grad lingers on the memory of long
vanished classmates, happy to recall their names even if he
didn't get on with them too well in the dear old days. As an
element of character delineation the passage is first-rate and
adds life to our picture of honorable old age, sentimental, wise,
reactionary, nostalgic, and, if it must be said, a little garrulous.
But is it poetry? Parodi[7] thinks it is and while recognizing, as
others have, the echo of Anchises' enumeration of illustrious
Romans in the sixth book of the *Aeneid*, suggests that we
might look at the passage as a kind of *sirventese*, that poetic
form characteristic of the Middle Ages in which elements of
chronicle or journalism and satire mingle. It has, indeed, many
of the components of a *sirventese*; the catalog, the specific
naming of names, and the biting lines, notably 105, describing
the Chiaramontesi as "those who yet blush for the bushel,"
and 114, with the sneer at the Visdomini and Tosinghi, "who
grow fat by staying in consistory." Bitter humor mingles with
outright censure, as should be the case in a good *sirventese*,
concluding, perhaps with a tone of grief a little too heavy for
the traditional form, in the allusion to the Buondelmonte
affair. I find it a passage full of Infernal memories; we could
easily imagine ourselves back in the lower kingdom. Many elements contribute to give this impression; the catalog itself reminds me a little of the report Dante gives Guido da Montefeltro on the state of affairs in Romagna. Del Lungo has seen in
the *nova fellonia* (new felony)—whatever it is—attributed to
the Cerchi, an echo of the *gente nuova* of Canto XVI of the
Inferno. And indeed the Infernal anti-Florentine thesis of new
people and quick money is latent in the discourse. The savage
satisfaction with which the fall of great families is remembered, "In what high state I saw them once whom now/ Pride
has undone," with reference to the Uberti (another Infernal
connection), recalls Virgil's mordant and somewhat vulgar
comment in *Inferno* VIII, "How many now account themselves as kings/ Who will yet wallow here like pigs in mire."
Then too the identification of some families by their stemma,

though it is a common enough device and one dear to the heraldic-conscious Cacciaguida, in this context makes one think of the usurers on the edge of the pit. Personal memories of the poet lurk behind some of his references and no doubt explain the vigor of his feelings; we shall note here only the allusion to the Adimari in verses 115–118, "The tribe intemperate, that like a dragon/ Harries those who flee, and grows meek as a lamb/ If any turn to show their teeth or purse." This is a bitter reference (to call on Del Lungo again) to the member of that family who had obtained the confiscation of our poet's personal property after his exile and incidentally once more suggests *Inferno* VIII, since Argenti was likewise a member of this insolent clan. And of course the double allusion to the statue of Mars (natural enough considering where we are) cannot but take our memories back to the dark wood of the suicides. A *sirventese* then. But its impact will depend somewhat on our knowledge of and passion for Florentine history.

We accept the point that like all prophets Dante is stressing his origin in an earthly community; he does seem however to document it too thoroughly. Some forty names crowded into sixty lines make a rather stiff dose and, truth to tell, are more suggestive of a tax list than of any verse form that comes readily to mind. This is not to deny the potential impact of this catalog on either professional historians or impassioned Florentines. I should love to have a tax list of two hundred years ago for my home town. I should find it enchanting, and Dante certainly has a right to his. Alas, I feel that this is his and not mine. I recall that Papini[8] once said no reader of the *Comedy* could fully appreciate its beauties unless he were a Florentine, a Catholic, and a poet. Unless we put a narrow definition on the word appreciate, I think this is untrue and an untruth that does much harm to Dante's greatness. I believe, with Lowell, that "to confine (his vision) to Florence or to Italy is to banish it from the sympathies of mankind." [9] But at certain moments in Canto XVI I can see what Papini meant.

I do find the catalog interesting in its relationship to other catalogs in the poem, of which there are many. There are catalogs of virtuous pagans, of ruling princes, of patriarchs, and, in the rose yet to come, another of princes and princesses of the faith. We had a kind of Florentine pocket catalog adumbrated in the sixth canto of the *Inferno* and brought to life in the sixteenth but hardly large enough to count as such. Sooner or later a larger edition was predictable, and of course this is the place for it. I wonder a little if it isn't put into the *Paradiso* to make up for the rather scanty number of Florentines who actually appear in the narrative. Outside of Beatrice and including Cacciaguida, there are only five fellow citizens of the poet's in the two realms of the saved and sainted, as against twenty-three in the *Inferno*. It has sometimes seemed to me that, in order to keep the proportions of his various quotas in some kind of syncretistic harmony, Dante used references and allusions to proper names to fill out the gaps in his presentation of *personae* of the narrative. For what it is worth I note, for example, that there are only two actual Old Testament characters among the denizens of Hell, but the number of those of such provenience *mentioned* there is strengthened by the catalog of the patriarchs. The same principle may be at work here.

If Cacciaguida is the heart of the *Paradiso*, Canto XVII is certainly the heart of the Cacciaguida episode. It is an extremely well-integrated unit, neither fragmented nor discursive, and I find its component parts in harmony with the underlying rule of three so characteristic of our poet's composition. The first part is introductory, setting forth Dante's state of mind and including Beatrice's exhortation to speak. In the second part Dante asks for and receives information about the pattern of his years to come. In the third part he seeks counsel on the nature of his poem and again receives straightforward advice. The presentation is not merely orderly but one might say psychologically human and natural.

Rather than follow the line of the poet's design here I should like to comment on one or two matters concerning the strategy of the canto and its implications. Many, indeed the majority of the commentators have noted that here Dante learns, as promised by Virgil in the *Inferno*, the course of his life, but, in spite of Virgil's specific assurance, he doesn't learn it from the lips of Beatrice but rather from Cacciaguida, whom Virgil seemed to know nothing of. I don't think this matters very much, but any inconsistency in Dante deserves our attention. As to why Cacciaguida speaks, Grabher[10] (again following Del Lungo) has I think the reasonable answer: these are earthly, familial, and to a certain extent even political matters, and it is appropriate they should be set forth by a man, a symbol, if you will, of the active life, rather than a girl transfigured into Revelation or whatever you choose to call Beatrice. Cosmo[11] is even more precise. Certainly the things Beatrice reveals should not be of quite the same order, and indeed they are not. All the prophecies given Dante which touch on the course of his life in this world are given him by men: Ciacco, Farinata, Brunetto, Malaspina, and so on; it is enough for Beatrice to assure him that he will be with her a *cive di quella Roma ove Cristo è romano* (citizen of that Rome wherein Christ is a Roman). This seems reasonable enough, but then we wonder why the poet ever suggested in the first place that this sort of information would come from Beatrice. Are we to see in this additional evidence that Virgil after all cannot know everything? Or did Dante change his mind somewhat about the rôle of Beatrice? Which would mean in turn that he not only wrote the *Inferno* before having the whole plan clearly in mind but also didn't have time to revise to make all the edges match. The double destiny of Manto would seem to indicate that such might well be the case. If we must at all costs make our poet consistent and infallible we can say that in a sense, since the whole journey is undertaken under Beatrice's sponsorship, everything he learns in the course of it comes through her, even if that isn't quite the way he puts it.

I cannot help commenting on the nature of the colloquy between Dante and his ancestor. One of the technical weapons of our poet is his able manipulation of dialog and conversation. Practically all the *Comedy* is in the form of dialog, which I have always thought was no small reason for its appeal, but the conversations vary enormously. One standard kind, what we might call the pupil-teacher kind, consists of Dante's asking a question and then submitting patiently to a disquisition on history, philosophy, theology, or whatever may be the case. This is indeed his normal form of exposition. But there are many conversations that are more truly dramatic than informational; an excellent example it seems to me is that between Dante and Farinata, in which both parties bear their share of the burden. It is usually with Florentines that Dante has this kind of conversation; I suppose for the obvious reason that the relationship is not pupil to teacher but peer to peer. In any event the talk with Cacciaguida is all but unique in that it blends both sorts. Mostly, to be sure, Cacciaguida speaks and Dante drinks in his discourse, but Dante has some words of his own and his personality has its own impact.

And here I should like to pick up a trifle that I find the commentators have somewhat neglected. Not all of them observe that the whole adventure of the journey is referred to three times in the course of this canto. In lines 19–21 Dante says:

> While I was yet in Virgil's company,
> Climbing the mountain cleansing to the soul
> And going down into the world of death . . .

He repeats the summary and indeed sharpens it in lines 112–115, no longer taking for granted his present situation:

> Down in the world of endless bitterness
> And on that mountain's side from whose fair peak
> My lady's eyes raised me aloft, and since . . .

Ultimately Cacciaguida picks up the theme in lines 136–137, reversing the time sequence of the journey:

Whence there have been shown you in these great wheels
And on the mount and in the vale of mourning.

Clearly the thought of his accomplishment in its detailed parts
was very much on Dante's mind. This summary, thrice uttered, is bound to remind us of the passage of Virgil's discourse in *Inferno* I, where a similar précis is given. It has here
too a little flavor of a formal farewell, something like the
thrice repeated "*Virgilio*" of *Purgatorio* xxx. But the *Comedy*
has sixteen cantos and yet another five heavens—counting the
Empyrean—to run. A little early for goodbyes? Yet there are
some finalities here. In what remains of his journey our wayfarer will see no other soul of what might be called the familial
circle. Nor will he have another opportunity to speak, within
the fabric of the narrative, of such matters as are touched on
here. Perhaps Professor Montano has put best what I am grop-
ing to say when he remarks that for all the weighty and beautiful things to follow, the rest of the *Paradiso* is in some sense
an epilogue; here is the *svolta* or turning point.[12]

In Canto XVIII Cacciaguida is in his last phase, and the
reader, after the earthly naturalistic framework of the great
conversation is back in a stylized, almost Byzantine paradise. If
Cacciaguida had reminded us a little of Brunetto Latini in
Canto XVII surely here he looks ahead to the rôle of St. Bernard in the last great splendors of the Empyrean. The reader,
who very likely has forgotten the great symbolic Cross and
the coruscant souls that compose it, is brought sharply back to
them. One authority well describes the gear shift here as "con-
tinuity of narrative and sudden change of tone." Actually I
think he might have said *resumption* of narrative, for in fact
the movement of the tale had drawn to a halt as we listened to
prophecy, exhortation, and counsel from the lips of the old
warrior. It has been remarked too, but perhaps not sufficiently
stressed, that there is also a change of linguistic color. The
simple, almost prose-like quality of the language that characterized the exchange of the two kinsmen is gone and the high

style is back again. In the first line we have the Latinism *verbo*,
and that is followed immediately by an elaborate compliment
to Beatrice, and, shortly after, one of Dante's numerous allusions to the metaphysical nature of Paradise, the tree that
draws its sustenance from the top. And obedient to Cacciaguida's signals the champions of God's warrior-class manifest
themselves in a kind of hierarchical formalism; "Perning in
their successive gyres" one might say, as the "singing master"
of Dante's soul points them out. Joshua and Judas Maccabee
get a terzina each, Charlemagne and Orlando share one, and
the fourth terzina encompasses the more recent or lesser figures of William of Orange and Reynouard, Godfrey of Bouillon and Robert Guiscard. The choice of the warrior souls
here displayed is not without interest. They make up, as Curtius reminds us,[13] another ennead, and their number suggests
the "nine worthies" of medieval tradition. Dante has taken
some liberties with the original cast of this heroic company.
The orthodox list appears in Caxton's preface to *Morte d'Arthur;* it contains three pagans, Hector, Alexander, and Julius
Caesar; three Jews, Joshua, David, and Judas Maccabaeus; and
three Christians, Arthur, Charlemagne, and Godfrey of Bouillon. Dante could not of course make any use of the pagan trio
in these exalted surroundings (all of whom have their place in
the *Inferno,* two in very respectable company); and of the
Jewish quota he will need David elsewhere. He retains the
other two Hebrews however and also two of the three Christian paladins, omitting only Arthur. He takes, in short, four of
the six available to him; with the vacancies left by the ineligi-
ble pagans he has scope for five choices of his own. Cacciaguida himself is one, and of the remaining four three are the
legendary paladins Roland, Reynouard and William of Orange; the Norman Robert Guiscard completes the muster. Roland is of course an inevitable selection, once the vacancy is
available, and perhaps one may say the same of William of
Orange. I am inclined to see in the choice of Reynouard a

gesture toward the first dislodged group—the pagans; for the legend tells us that Reynouard was born a Saracen; and in Robert Guiscard, true champion of the Church that he was, a like gesture toward the House of Swabia, since he was the founder of the Sicilian line. Perhaps Dante regards him as the Italian counterpart of Godfrey; in any event his historical rôle from the point of view of an Italian is sufficient to justify his inclusion. They are all, of course, Crusaders—which, I suppose, is why Arthur is passed over.

But is it indeed an ennead? Do we not rather see here ten devoted soldiers of the Cross? Father Foster, in his recent essay, "Chivalry and Dante," sharpens what seems to me the very valid point, made by some other critics, that the poet himself is "a crusader too, though his weapon is not the sword but language and his enemy not the Saracen but a degenerate Christendom." [14] Certainly no crusader was ever assigned a mission clearer and loftier than that given to Dante here.

Having now done his duty as guide, as he had that as counselor, Cacciaguida joins the other paladins, adds his voice to their song, and takes his leave of Dante and the poem. We are at line 51, marking what one commentator[15] calls the caesura of the canto, the fifth in which Cacciaguida has had a part.

Let us now look back—*suole a riguardar giovar altrui* (for one may profit from a backward glance)—and see what kind of light Mars has given us. First of all the pilgrim Dante has been given the clearest illumination provided for him in the *Comedy*. At the beginning Virgil told him that the journey was to be undertaken for his own good; his words in the opening canto disclosed nothing of the missionary aspect of the enterprise. Beginning with *Inferno* IX, where the poet had charged "healthy intellects" to ponder his meaning, the idea of what we may call public service comes into the poem: Beatrice most specifically charges the pilgrim in Canto XXXIII of the *Purgatorio* to take back messages to the land of the living for the general profit of mankind. But nowhere before has the missionary purpose of the poem been so clearly set forth; we now know that it is meant to be "vital nutriment" for its readers. And what is meant for the traveller is also meant for the poet, for of course Cacciaguida is Dante's other self. In Mars, I think, pilgrim and poet are one—in a sense which obtains rarely elsewhere, perhaps only in the final vision.

But the light from Mars is shed most copiously on the reader. In many respects the Cacciaguida episode is the most illuminating of the *Comedy*. Let us enjoy first of all the glow of the valiant Crusader himself, simply as another creation within the poem. From a dramatic point of view he is unforgettably realized and, developed as he is at a more leisurely tempo and with more varied facets than any other character that comes to mind, he may claim to rank with Francesca, Farinata, Ugolino, and the like, viewed simply as a vigorously depicted member of the *dramatis personae*. But this is accomplished without the use of any naturalistic detail; Heaven being what it is and the souls mere radiations of light, Dante cannot use any such phrases as he employed to indicate the posture of Farinata or the scorched aspect of Brunetto or even the wasted features of Forese. Yet somehow he gives plastic and visual life to his character. I think it is because of the suggestions implicit in the lines assigned to the old Crusader. He has not only the Ghibelline arrogance of Farinata, the fatherly affection of Brunetto, and something of Virgil's sagacity, he has also, with his dignity and open speech, a little of Cato's austerity. Perhaps in Cacciaguida's suggestion of the poet's ultimate triumph there is even a reminiscence of Charon's assurance, however gruffly expressed, of Dante's happy destiny. He is, in a word, the definitive edition of the father image, which is one of the persistent archetypes of the poem from Virgil to San Bernardo.

And he brings together too in his own person a number of the leitmotivs of the *Comedy*. In him harmoniously concur the old Florentine motif, the Ghibelline thread, and the prophetic strain. Like Farinata, Brunetto, and Beatrice, he is given the respectful *voi*.

More than that, he serves to unify, as no other character in the poem does, the great axes of Church and State, Cross and Eagle, as Valli saw them. For Mars is dominated by the great Cross, but it was in the service of the Imperial Eagle that Cacciaguida met his death. In the perfect world of a virtuous and simple Florence, of crusading Emperors and honest Popes, Cross and Eagle are united—as they are in Heaven. Not for nothing is Charlemagne cited first among the Christians, not for nothing does Dante's great-great-grandsire insist that his mother was a saint and that he was born a Christian and Cacciaguida. We have seen how his salutation brings our poet's mission into relationship with that of Aeneas, Paul, and something even more exalted. And in his final charge to his beloved "son" Cacciaguida discloses not only the character of the mission but the nature of the means to be employed, the plan of the sacred book itself. It is to deal with lofty personalities, a prescription if not tragic at least aristocratic, but the language he himself employs and which is suggested for the poem is to be straightforward, open, and vernacular. For these lofty examples are to be put, as it were, to public service, and if the cast of characters is aristocratic the message is for Everyman.

I cannot forbear to add a further word about the language of this particular episode, since I am treating it as a kind of biopsy of the *Commedia*. Vossler found Cacciaguida a determinant or a revelation of the style of the poem; he is "the spring, so to speak, out of which the sacred poison of satire flows through the whole *Comedy*." [16] But I am interested here more in the color of this passage itself than in its prescription for that of the *Comedy* as a whole. To me it seems that all the styles of the various realms are present in this section. I have mentioned the Infernal tone of certain lines, and surely the unforgettable phrase "and let them scratch wherever is the itch" is a fair example; it would not have been inappropriate on the lips of Ciacco. I find a suggestion of the pastoral and very human poetry of the *Purgatorio* in the lines recalling the untroubled life of old Florence, typified, let us say, by the terzina:

> Florence, within the old encircling walls
> whence even now she takes her tierce and nones
> contained herself in peace, sober and chaste.
>
> (XV, 97–99)

And of course the colors of Paradisiac glory are with us, particularly in the introduction and end of the episode, with its ruby glowing Cross and saintly soldiers in their "kinetic ballet," to borrow a phrase from a Russian poet.[17] The ornament too is rich; I shall mention only the comparison to the Milky Way, the magic naturalism of the motes of dust dancing in the sunbeam of a darkened room, and the beautifully realistic— but with a heavenly realism—figure of the torch seen through alabaster. There is a rather large number of words found nowhere else in the *Comedy*, the color words *robbi* and *lucore*, as also *deturpa, insusi,* and *tetragono.*

But of course the golden kernel of the Cacciaguida episode, and the reason why it has been quite correctly seen as the most moving and significant passage in the *Comedy* is the portrait of Dante that emerges from it. Many critics more subtle than I have lingered lovingly and perceptively over this self-portrait, which tells us more of the author than perhaps he meant us to know. I shall limit my comments to four unforgettable terzinas. Warning him of his exile, Cacciaguida tells our poet:

> You will abandon everything you love
> Most dearly, this is but the arrow first
> Discharged by exile's bow: thereafter too
> You shall yet learn how salty to the taste
> Is alien bread, and come to feel how hard
> Another's stairs are to descend or mount.
>
> (XVII, 55–60)

Striking is the passage from the general to the precisely particular. In the phrase "everything you love most dearly" we can almost feel the utter despair, the moment of stunned realization that our whole little cosmos has been swept away. The very lack of particularization bespeaks this all but inarticulate anguish. No need to ask *what* is held most dear; at such a moment one hardly knows: wife, family, friends, the familiar circle, the streets, the buildings, even, it may be, the soft Tuscan air, of which Dante speaks elsewhere. Then, hard upon it, the specific. Was the bread of Verona truly more salty; were there real staircases he had in mind or is the word brought in by the rhyme and meant merely to suggest the humble things of daily life? Both, I have always thought, and, as for the latter reference, it is not hard to picture the proud postulant laboring up successive stairways to the *piano signorile* to present his petition and reveal his need to various of the high and mighty, secure in their own domestic comfort. More generally, in the reference to bread, I feel the nostalgia for the simple things of home has never been better put. One does not need to be a political exile but merely a homesick traveller to know that for all its glamor you can't get a real American hamburger on the Via Veneto or, on the other side, for all the Italian infiltration into the American stream of life, a lonesome Roman in Chicago will look in vain for the authentic *cannelloni*, the true *abbacchio*. Dante's sensitivity and warm emotional responsiveness are apparent here as nowhere else in the Comedy.

And then the shocking and revealing bitterness of what follows:

> And what shall heaviest weigh your shoulders down
> Will be the company of fools and rogues
> With whom you shall descend into this vale,
> For ingrates all, and impious and mad
> They'll turn on you, but in short course of time
> *They and not you will bear the temples red.*
>
> (*Ibid.*, 61–66)

This is the ferociously self-righteous partisan, this is the Dante who could address his fellow citizens as "crazy by nature and crazy by corruption"; who, in the shrewd hypothesis of Carducci,[18] so terrified the boy Petrarch as to condition forever the nature of the admiration the latter was to hold for him; who could take even God Almighty to task for permitting the mismanagement of Italy.

Only such a man, at once, to use his own words, *transmutabile* (impressionable) by temperament and *tetragono* (unshakable) in character, could have had both the understanding and the self-assurance to undertake the mission overtly assigned him here; only such a man, as we see him finally illuminated by his own words against the Cross of Mars, could have made his own life into a universal allegory, reading the eternal into the contingent; only such a man could have written the *Comedy*.

Notes

I have had occasion in the course of these essays to refer to the follow-ing modern commentaries of the *Comedy:* T. Cassini—S. Barbi, 6th Ed. (Florence, 1926); S. Chimenz (Turin, 1963); I. Del Lungo (Florence, 1926); A. Momigliano (Florence, 1948); L. Pietrobono (Turin, 1923–1926); D. Provenzal, 2d. Ed. (Florence, 1926); N. Sapegno (Florence, 1955–1957); G. A. Scartazzini, 2d. Ed. (Milan, 1896); F. Torraca, 5th Ed. (Milan-Rome-Naples, 1921); E. Trucchi, *Esposizione della Divina commedia* (Milan, 1936). Since in all cases the context will indicate under what line or passage the glosses referred to may be found I have not thought it necessary to indicate them by a footnote.

Chapter 3. Citizen Dante

1. Original in Jacopone da Todi, *Laudi, trattato e detti,* ed. by Franca Ageno (Florence, 1953), no. XLVIII, p. 192.
2. From *Rime,* CCLIX.
3. *Cronica,* IX, 136.
4. *Il poeta e il politico e altri saggi* (Milan, 1960), p. 53.
5. *Vita nouva,* XLI. Translation by Thomas Okey in Temple Classics Edition (London, 1906), pp. 145–147.
6. *Convivio* IV, xxiv, 12.
7. *Ibid.,* XXVIII, 3. Translation by Philip Wicksteed in Temple Classics Edition (London, 1903), p. 371.
8. *Convivio* IV, iv, 2–4. Wicksteed's translation, p. 242.
9. *Ibid.,* IV, vii, 9. Pp. 260–261.

Chapter 4. Hell: Topography and Demography

1. *Further Papers on Dante* (New York, 1957), p. 2.
2. L. Malagoli, *Saggio sulla Divina Commedia* (Florence, 1962), p. 17.
3. "Dante," *The Poet and the Politician* (Carbondale, Ill., 1964), p. 77.

4. See Julius Wilhelm, "Zum Problem der schönen Lanschaft in Der Divina Commedia," *Dante-Jahrbuch*, XXXIX (1963), 63–79.
5. *The Treatment of Nature in Dante's "Divina Commedia,"* (London–New York, 1897), p. 51.
6. See "Notes of a lecture on Donne, Dante and Milton, delivered Feb. 27, 1818," in *"Dante" in Notes and Letters upon Shakespeare and Some of the Old Poets*, ed. by Mrs. H. N. Coleridge (New York, 1953).
7. *European Literature and the Latin Middle Ages* (New York, 1953), p. 365.
8. It is impossible to be precise on the classical figures. Is the daughter of Tiresias (*Purg*. XXII, 113) firmly to be identified with Manto? And even the omniscient Pauly cannot tell how many were the sisters of Deidamia (line 114). I may add that in my Roman census I include Livy; with the encouragement of Momigliano and some of the older commentators I dare think he is a more likely reference than Linus (in *Inf*. IV, 141).
9. Curtius, *European Literature*, pp. 368–371.

Chapter 5.   Women of the *Comedy*

1. Original in Alfred Jeanroy, *Les Chansons de Guillaume X* (Paris, 1932), pp. 22–23.
2. *Summa Theologiae* I, Qu. 92, A. 1.
3. *De remediis utriusque fortunae* II, 17.
4. *Opere volgari*, ed. by Cecil Grayson (Bari, 1966), II, 129.
5. H. Hatzfeld, in *Letture dantesche*, ed. by G. Getto (Florence, 1962), p. 784.
6. Edmund Gardner, *Dante's Ten Heavens*, 2d. Ed. (London, 1904), p. 95.
7. "Francesca da Rimini"; I quote here the English version of Joseph Rossi and Alfred Galpin in their *De Sanctis on Dante* (Madison, Wis., 1957), p. 39.
8. "The Meaning of Heaven and Hell" in her *Introductory Papers on Dante* (New York, 1954), p. 80.

Chapter 6.   Dante's Provençal Gallery

1. A. G. Ferrers Howell's translation; see *Dante's Latin Works*, Temple Classics Edition (London, 1904), p. 71.
2. A. Momigliano, *Purgatorio* (Florence, 1948)), note on Canto XXVIII, lines 127–129, p. 209.
3. V. Crescini, *"Inferno—Canto XXVIII"* in *Letture dantesche*, ed. by G. Getto (Florence, 1962), p. 563.
4. See, among others, H. A. Pochmann's articles: "Irving's German Sources in the Sketch Book," *Studies in Philology*, XXVIII (July, 1930), 477–507, and "Irving's German Tour and Its Influence on His Tales," *PMLA*, XLV (Dec., 1930), 1150–1187.
5. See Ananda K. Coomaraswamy, "Headless Magicians; and an Act of Truth," *Journal of the American Oriental Society*, Vol. 64 (1944), 215–217.
6. S. Santangelo, *Dante e i trovatori provenzali*, 2d. Ed. (Catania, 1959), Chapter V.
7. In his note on *Inferno* XXVIII, 134, *Divina Commedia* (Florence, 1881).

8. *Personae*, New Directions (New York, 1949), p. 36.
9. In his note to xxvıı, line 7, *Inferno* (Florence, 1955).
10. See "Bertran de Born" in *Poesia antica e moderna* (Bari, 1943), p. 143.
11. André Pézard in his note in *Romania*, 78 (1957), 519–524, comments on such hypotheses, adding his own for good measure.
12. See "Dante and Arnaut Daniel" by C. M. Bowra in *Speculum* XXVII (1952), 460–461.
13. *Arnaut Daniel: Canzoni* (Florence, 1960), pp. 99–106.
14. Charles H. Grandgent, *Divine Comedy*, Rev. Ed. (Boston, 1933), p. 561.
15. Bowra, "Dante and Arnaut Daniel," p. 474.
16. The essay on Arnaut Daniel may be found in *The Literary Essays of Ezra Pound* (London, 1954), pp. 109–148.
17. A. Del Monte, *Studi sulla poesia ermetica medievale* (Naples, 1953), p. 95.
18. N. Sapegno, *Purgatorio* (Florence, 1956), note on xxvı, 140.
19. G. A. Scartazzini, *La Divina Commedia*, 2d. Ed. (Milan, 1896); note on *Par.* ıx, lines 64–108.
20. S. Stroński, *Folquet de Marseille* (Cracow, 1910), pp. *99–*100.
21. *Ibid.*, p. *66.
22. H. J. Chaytor, *Troubadours of Dante* (Oxford, 1902), p. 142.
23. See Cesare de Lollis, "Quel di Lemosi" in his *A Ernesto Monaci per l'anno XXV del suo insegnamento* (Rome, 1901), p. 364.
24. Santangelo, *Dante e i trovatori*, p. 118.
25. *Ibid.*, p. 129.
26. Mario Apollonio, *Dante: Storia della Commedia*, 2d. Ed. (Milan, 1954), Vol. II, p. 810.
27. G. Gentile, "Purgatorio—Canto vı" in *Letture dantesche*.
28. See Marco Boni, *Sordello, le poesie* (Bologna, 1954), pp. xiii–ciii.
29. *Ibid.*, ci–ciii.
30. Alessandro D'Ancona, "Purgatorio vıı" in *Letture dantesche*.
31. Translation by A. G. Ferrers Howell, Temple Classics Edition (London, 1904).
32. In the Temple Classics Edition of *Dante's Latin Works*, p. 51.
33. A. Marigo's edition of the *De vulgari eloquentia* (Florence, 1938), p. 126n.
34. G. Bertoni, in *Giornale storico della letteratura italiana*, XXVIII (1901), 269 ff.
35. See Boni's *Sordello*, 279–281 for text; cix–cx for comment
36. See F. Torraca's "Sul Sordello di Cesare de Lollis" in *Giornale dantesco*, IV (1897), 42.
37. Boni, *Sordello*, p. clxxiv.
38. P. E. Guarnerio in *Giornale storico della letteratura italiana*, XXVIII (1896), 383.
39. C. M. Bowra, "Dante and Sordello" in his *General and Particular* (Cleveland-New York, 1964), pp. 113–114.
40. See the *cobla* "No·m meraveil si·l marit son gilos" in Boni's *Sordello*, p. 195.
41. See F. Flamini, "Nel cielo di Venere" in *Varia* (Leghorn, 1905), pp. 95–96.
42. *Letterature d'oc e d'oil*, 2d. Ed. (Milan, 1955), pp. 441–442.
43. Cf. the *Cansos* "Bel m'es" and "Tant m'abellis," respectively IV and XI in Boni's edition.

Chapter 7. *Paradiso* IX

1. F. Flamini, "Nel Cielo di Venere," in *Varia* (Leghorn, 1905), p. 108.
2. The daughter does not lack defenders. Lana, Buti, l'Anonimo, and Landino among the ancients, Scartazzini, Torraca, Trucchi, Casini, and Flamini in *Nel Cielo* so interpret *tuo*. For the wife: Pietro di Dante, Benvenuto, and Serravalle, and among the moderns, aside from those quoted in the text, also Dino Provenzal and Siro Chimenz; Pietrobono seems undecided. We may add that the *Ottimo commento* believes Dante is addressing the mother of Charles. Scartazzini's rebuttal, that Charles's mother's name was not Clemenza but Maria, does not entirely dispose of the matter; if the *Ottimo* could confuse the names perhaps Dante could too. But it seems unlikely; I am content with the reasoning of Del Lungo and Momigliano.
3. Flamini, "Nel Cielo," p. 86, says firmly: *qui non si tratta d'una profezia a posteriori!* (here there is no question of a prophecy to posterity).
4. In Dante's time Ezzelino had already become a legendary figure of monstrous evil. Most of the accounts of his deeds are based on the chronicle of Rolandino; see E. Kantorowicz, *Frederick the Second* (New York, 1957), pp. 612–613. How much of this black legend Dante believed is hard to say. He treats Ezzelino very lightly; the phrase applied to him in *Inferno* x is purely descriptive (see G. Secrétant *Il canto IX del Paradiso*, Florence, 1911, p. 14) and not necessarily derogatory; and, as Flamini points out, the "firebrand" may apply only to the legendary dream of Ezzelino's mother. Yet unquestionably Dante accepted the common view that he was an evil tyrant, for in Hell, after all, he is. To a certain extent, too, our poet at least recognized the truth of the reputation of Cunizza, else he would not have conceded that her presence in Paradise would cause wonder among the *vulgo*. In the one case he follows the popular verdict, in the other he rejects it—for his own sentimental or artistic reasons. It is hard to agree with Secrétant (p. 19) that Dante "neither loved nor admired Cunizza." Souls beloved by our poet may get into the *Inferno;* none that he despises or dislikes wins his way to Heaven.
5. *The Ottimo commento della Divina commedia* (Pisa, 1827–1829, Vol. 3, p. 223) remarks that the contrasting fates of Cunizza and her brother illustrate Charles Martel's comment at the end of Canto VIII.
6. Marco Boni, *Sordello, le poesie* (Bologna, 1954), pp. 29–38.
7. Flamini, "Nel Cielo" (pp. 95–96), dwells extensively on the impression that the old Signora, passing her declining years in the house of the Cavalcanti, may have made on the young poet.
8. And the good delight in hearing of the wicked things of their past, which no longer pertain to them; they delight not because such things are wicked but because they were and are no more. *Confessions* X, iii.
9. Even though Flamini reminds us that *indulgo* may simply mean *concedo*, the substance is not really altered. Chimenz' *condono* (condone) seems the accurate verb here.
10. It is interesting to note that in the only other case (*Par.* XXII, 28), it is used to modify *margherita*. Dante evidently associated the word with jewels.
11. Cf. *Convivio* II, xv, 115–118: "We are already in the final age of the

world, and are indeed awaiting the consummation of the celestial movement." Flamini, in "Nel Cielo" (p. 101), believes that Dante's line here represents his precise estimate of the time left to mankind; Scartazzini, however, citing a host of commentators, sees the statement as merely an indeterminate prophecy.

12. E. Trucchi, pp. 138–139, summarizes the matter very well; ultimately the source is Ferreto de Ferreti; see Ludovicus Muratori: *Rerum Italicarum scriptores* X, 1065 *sq.*

13. *Cf.* Ferreto in Muratori: *Rerum Italicarum* XII, 783 *sq.*

14. The *Ottimo* comments, p. 227, "Ah shameful gift and unbecoming a priest, an unspeakable cruelty—to hand over thirteen free Christians to murderers!"

15. Pietrobono well remarks that the existence of three such places with the same name is sufficient argument to conclude that "Malta" might be applied to any dank and dark prison. *Cf.* Flamini, "Nel Cielo," p. 100, also V. Cian, "La malta dantesca" in *Atti della R. Accademia delle scienze di Torino*, XXIX (1894), and M. Antonelli in *Giornale storico della letteratura italiana* LXXVII (1921), 150–152.

16. I cannot agree with Sapegno that *giù* means on earth; Dante has already used *qui* to signify our mortal life, and the employment of another adverb in the same sense and in juxtaposition would be unnecessarily clumsy. Provenzal observes: "In one single terzina the poet describes the two manifestations of joy: the heavenly and the earthly, and the expression of grief—for there can be no joy down there—characteristic of Hell."

17. Erich von Richthofen, *Veltro und Diana* (Tübingen, 1956), p. 103, cites thirteen verbs created by Dante on the roots of pronouns, adverbs, numerals, etc. All are from the *Paradiso;* five from the sphere of Venus and four of those from our canto. No other canto has so many.

18. *Cf.* M. Casella, "Questioni di geografia dantesca," *Studi danteschi* XII, 1927.

19. *La personalità storica di Folchetto di Marsiglia nella Commedia* (Bologna, 1897). But Torraca ("A proposito di Folchetto," *Nuovi Studi danteschi* (Naples, 1921), p. 483) reminds us that "The fire of love burns in countless poems whether written by Provençals or others——and with greater sincerity of expression." One may remark too that, although Folquet's poetry is characterized by classical references and phrases (*cf.* S. Stroński, *Le Troubadour Folquet de Marseille*, Cracow, 1910, pp. 75–87), it is Dante who gives him Dido, Phyllis, and Iole, none of whom are mentioned in Folquet's extant works.

20. For the details of Folquet's life and the character of his muse, see Stroński, my authority unless otherwise noted.

21. *Cf.* note 9 above.

22. *Cf.* P. Toynbee, *Dante Studies and Researches* (London, 1902), p. 72.

23. Toynbee, in *Dante Studies,* p. 288, reminds us that "by the Fathers Rahab was regarded as the type of the Church, the 'line of scarlet thread' which she bound in her window (Josh. ii, 21) being typical of the blood of Christ shed for the remission of sins"; he cites Isidore of Seville and Peter Comestor on the subject, as authorities with whose works Dante was familiar.

24. Zingarelli, *La personalità storica,* pp. 27–31.

25. *Cf.* M. Porena, in *Rassegna,* Anno XXXII, no. 4–5 (1924) and the comment of G. Vandelli in *Studi danteschi* X (1925), 141.

26. F. d'Ovidio in *Studi danteschi sulla Divina commedia* (Milan-Palermo, 1901), p. 391n.
27. Guilhem Figueira, "*D'un sirventes far*" in V. de Barthlomeis, *Poesie provenzali storiche* (Rome, 1931).
28. Karl Vossler, *Mediaeval Culture* (New York, 1929), II, 371.

Chapter 8. Light from Mars

1. *Letture dantesche*, ed. by G. Getto (Florence, 1962), p. 1633.
2. Umberto Cosmo, *L'ultima ascesa*, 2d. Ed. (Florence, 1965).
3. E. R. Curtius, *European Literature and the Latin Middle Ages* (New York, 1953), p. 360.
4. J. A. Mazzeo, "Dante and the Pauline Modes of Vision" in his *Structure and Thought in the Paradise* (Ithaca, 1958), pp. 102–103.
5. *Symbolism in Medieval Thought and Its Consummation in the Divine Comedy*, New Ed. (New York, 1961), pp. 65–68.
6. E. Donadoni in *Letture dantesche*, p. 1652.
7. E. G. Parodi in *Letture dantesche*, p. 1670.
8. Giovanni Papini, *Dante vivo* (Florence, 1933), p. 14.
9. James Russell Lowell, *Among My Books*, 2d. Series (Boston, 1876), p. 93.
10. Carlo Grabher in *Letture dantesche*, p. 1681.
11. Cosmo, *L'ultima ascesa*, pp. 169–170.
12. Rocco Montano, *Storia della poesia di Dante* (Naples, 1963), II, 488.
13. Curtius, *European Literature*, p. 372.
14. K. Foster, "Chivalry and Dante," in his *God's Tree* (London, 1957), p. 167.
15. G. B. Squarotti in *Letture dantesche*, p. 1710.
16. Karl Vossler, *Mediaeval Culture*, Reprint (New York, 1958), p. 169.
17. Osip Mandelshtam, "Talking about Dante," in *A Homage to Dante, Books Abroad* (Norman, Okla., 1965), p. 43.
18. C. Carducci, "Sulla varia fortuna di Dante in Italia," in *Studi letterari* (Leghorn, 1874), pp. 339–340.

Index

Abati family, 58
Abruzzi, Italy, 104
Acheron, river of Hell, 12, 50, 52
Achilles, 12
Achitophel, 92
Adam, 15, 17, 68, 70, 137
Adamo, Maestro, 56, 57, 62
Adige river, 123
Adimari family, 155
Aeneas, 35, 36; Dante identification
    with, 148, 149, 150, 151, 163
Aeneid (Virgil), 9, 154
Age, virtues of, 35
Albert I of Austria, king of Ger-
    many, 5
Alberti family, 62, 81
Alberti, Leon Battista, quoted, 68
Albigensian (Catharist) heresy, 9,
    97–98, 133–34
Alcides, 99, 132
Al cor gentil ripara sempre amore
    (Guinizelli), 13
Alexander the Great, 3, 57, 160
Alfraganus, 137
Ali, Caliph, 88
Aliscamps, 52
Allegory, correspondences and, 110–
    111, 120; Martian, 145–46, 150, 163;
    personal, 18, 22–23, 30, 102, 148–
    149, 150–51, 155, 156, 164–66; real-
    ism and, 15, 48, 64, 157; of salva-
    tion, 10, 16–17, 19–20, 21, 45–46, 49,
    50, 65, 101, 112, 137

Almerico di Braganza, 120
Altaforte, 92
Ambition, sin of, 14, 15
Anastasius, pope, 60
Anchises, 148, 149, 150, 154
Ancona, Alessandro d', cited, 107,
    110
Andrew the Chaplain, 67
Anglade, J., 105
Annas, 60
"Anonimo fiorentino, L'," cited, 74
Antenor, 58, 126
Apollonio, Mario, quoted, 102
Apulia, 54
Arabs, 60
Ar auziretz encabalitz cantars (Gui-
    raut de Bornelh), 100
Argenti, Filippo, 155
Aristocracy, 40–42, 115–16, 123, 163;
    Dante and, 4, 26, 32, 41, 43–44, 60–
    61, 124–25; religion and, 9; Sor-
    dello and, 42, 103, 105, 107, 109
Aristotle, 9, 33
Arms, *see* War
Arnaut Daniel, *see* Daniel, Arnaut
Arno river, 139
Arthur, King, 160, 161
Aruns, 59
Ascetic tradition, 25–26, 45
Asdente, 61
Astronomy, 137, 141, 145–46; Milky
    Way and, 150, 164
Athamas, 1

Attila, 60
Augustine, saint, 81, 121
Augustus Caesar, death of, 145
Avarice, 18, 52, 122; of the Church, 97, 139–41; Florentine, 154; women and, 60, 71, 76
Avignon, France: papacy in, 8, 9, 141

Bacchiglione river, 124
Barbi, T., cited, 105
Barral, Lord, 133
Bartoli, Adolfo, quoted, 97
Battaglia, S., cited, 91
Beatrice Portinari, 26, 28, 37, 44–46, 47, 65, 71, 160; as revelation, 101, 157; Cacciaguida and, 143, 145, 148, 152, 156, 157, 158, 161–62; on the City of Paradise, 35; the *Convivio* and, 101; Dante on the death of, 32–33; Hell and, 60, 62; on the rising soul, 19, 20–21; narrative uses of, 10, 11, 18, 23, 30, 36, 118, 130, 157, 158
Belacqua, 4, 147
Belus, 99, 132
Benevento, battle of, 104
Benvenuto da Imola, cited, 51, 61, 74, 105, 138; quoted, 82, 98, 121
Bernard, saint, 162; narrative use of, 11, 37, 111, 159
Be·m platz lo gais temps de pascor (Bertran de Born), 91
Bertoni, G., 107
Bertran de Born, *see* Born, Bertran de
Bianchi, Brunone, 81
Binyon, Laurence, quoted, 52
Bishop of Toulouse, *see* Folquet de Marseille
Blacatz, Sordello's lament for, 103, 107, 109, 110
Boccaccio, Giovanni, 3, 26, 120
Bolgia, *see* Malebolge
Bologna, Italy, 56, 57, 59; language of, 106
Bolsena, Lake, 125
Boni, Marco, cited, 103–104, 107, 108, 109
Boniface VIII, pope, 62, 98, 141
Born, Bertran de, 21, 60, 87, 88–93, 96, 134; Sordello and, 81, 109, 129

Bornelh, Guiraut de, 87, 99–100, 101
Bougia, Italy, 131, 132
Bowra, C. M., cited, 96, 108; quoted, 94–95
Brenta river, 53, 55, 80, 119
Brescia, Italy, 106, 107
Brunetto Latini, *see* Latini, Brunetto
Brutus, 56
Buiamonte, Giovanni, 62
Buondelmonte, "Mosca," 154
Buti, Francesco, cited, 117, 135

Cacciaguida, 37, 44, 60, 85, 89, 93, 138, 143–66; Florence and, 4, 19, 38, 146, 148, 151–56, 162–63
Caccianemico, Venedico, 58
Cagnano river, 124, 125
Caiaphas, 60
Caina, 12, 58, 84
Cammino, Gherardo da, 81, 125
Cammino, Riccardo da, 81, 125, 126
Can Grande (Can Francesco della Scala), 10, 124, 150
Canon law (Decretals), 97, 140
Capaneus, 62, 64
Capocchio, 2
Carducci, G., cited, 8, 166
Carlo Roberto (Charles I, king of Hungary), 116
Casella, 147
Casentino, 56
Casini, S., cited, 105
Cassius, 56
Catalano de' Malavolti, 62
Cathari, *see* Albigensian heresy
Catholicism, 7, 44, 155; *cefalofori* and, 88; characterization and, 15, 101, 134, 137–38, 151; crusades and, 97–98, 133–34, 138, 139–40, 163; medieval, 25–26, 31, 45, 52; state power and, 8–9, 27, 30, 39, 40, 141, 163; view of salvation in, 16, 19–21, 45, 46, 121; view of women in, 67
Cato, 4, 62, 110–11, 162
Cavalcanti family, 58
Cavalcanti, Cavalcante, 11
Caxton, William, 160
Celestinus, saint, 98
Centaurs, 61, 63
Cerchi family, 154
Certaldo, Italy, 38

Chanson de la Croisade, 133–34
Charlemagne, 160, 163
Charles I (Carlo Roberto), king of Hungary, 116
Charles II, king of Naples, 24
Charles of Anjou, 27, 104
Charles Martel, king of Hungary and prince of Naples and Sicily, 18, 79, 81, 113, 114, 118, 127, 130, 136; on hereditary virtue, 24, 42–43, 115–16, 120, 151; prophecy of, 116–17, 139, 140
Charles of Valois, 146, 153
Charon, 61, 162
Chaytor, H. J., 90; quoted, 100
Chiaramontesi family, 154
Christ, *see* Jesus Christ
Christianity, *see* Catholicism
Church, The, *see* Catholicism
Ciacco, 52, 62, 63, 147, 157, 163; on Florentine politics, 37
Ciampolo, 61
Cicero, "Dream of Scipio" of, 148
Cincinnatus, 152
Cino of Pistoia, 87
Classicism, 9, 44, 59, 63, 70; Florentine virtues and, 152; golden age legend and, 17; Judaeo-Christian tradition and, 3, 56–57, 60; monster figures and, 61; "sweet new style" and, 93
Clemence of Hapsburg, queen of Naples, 115, 116
Clement V, pope, 62
Cleopatra, 12, 14, 59, 70
Cocytus, 49, 60, 61, 62, 81
Coleridge, Samuel Taylor, quoted, 55
Confessions (Augustine), 81
Constance of Sicily, Holy Roman Empress, 21, 122; Piccarda and, 77–79, 80, 110
Constantine I, emperor of Rome and Byzantium, 141
Conti Guidi family, 58
Convivio (Dante Alighieri), 28, 30, 47; on Bertran de Born, 89; on Divine Justice, 127; on hereditary power, 41, 108; instructive purpose of, 5, 29, 33–35, 101, 108; on Mars, 145–46; on poetry, 10; on social good, 39–40

Cornelia, 152
Cosmo, Umberto, 144, 157
Cremona, Italy, 106, 107
Crescini, V., cited, 88, 89
Croce, Benedetto, 145; quoted, 91
Crusades, 133–34; Cacciaguida and, 19, 143, 146, 151, 152, 161, 162; papal reluctance for, 97–98, 138, 139–40
Cunizza da Romano, 18–19, 79–82, 84–85, 97, 113, 114, 130, 132, 134, 139, 140, 151; abduction of, 81, 104, 108–109, 120–21, 122; introduction of, 118–19; vocabulary of, 99, 102, 115, 123–26, 135
Curio, Gaius Scribonius, 3, 57, 88
Curtius, Ernst Robert, 56, 63, 148, 160

Damiano, Pietro, quoted, 140
Daniel, Arnaut, 21, 81, 87, 100, 127; style of, 93–96, 99, 101, 134
Dante Alighieri, 3, 7, 10, 26–46; biographical facts, 8–9, 26–28, 153; Cacciaguida and, 143–66; early works, 26, 28–29, 134; as narrative character, 11, 15–18, 19, 20, 21, 22–23, 36, 49–55, 57, 72, 102, 118, 129, 130, 145, 146, 147–48, 149–51, 156, 157, 161–63, 164–66; Provençal influences on, 87–111, 134, 154, 155; women and, 65–86, 152, 153
Danube river, 56
David, King, 141, 150, 160
Decretals (canon law), 97, 140
Della Fontana family, 125
Del Lungo, I., cited, 116, 154, 155, 157
Del Monte, A., quoted, 95
Democracy, 4, 5, 8, 123, 163; hermeticism and, 32–33; political, 40, 41, 43, 44, 123–24
Demophoön, 99, 132
Denis, saint, 88
De Sanctis, Francesco, quoted, 83
Despair, sin of, 15
Didacticism, 3, 4, 9, 23, 36, 48, 85, 87, 145, 161–62; of the *Convivio*, 29, 33–35, 101, 108; *cortegiano* tradition, 108; dialog and, 158; love and, 13–14, 97–102; political, 5, 8, 14–15, 35, 37, 39, 47, 97–98, 113, 121

Dido, 3, 12, 59, 70; Folquet and, 133, 134

Diomed, 62

Dionysius the Areopagite, 127

Dis, 61, 62

Discord, sowers of, 21, 39, 54, 88, 109

Divine Comedy, The (Dante Alighieri), the *Convivio* and, 29, 30, 47, 101; diversity of, 3–5, 9, 10–11, 30–31, 49, 56–57; purposes of, 3, 9–10, 35–36, 37, 47, 57, 85, 102, 115, 144, 150, 161–62, 163, 166; role of Dante in, 16 (*See also* Dante Alighieri, as narrative character); role of Mars in, 143–66; role of Venus in, 112–42, 144; troubadour tradition and, 87–111, 127; women of, 65–86

Doglia mi reca (Dante), 100

Dominic, saint, 120

Donadoni, E., cited, 84*n*, 153

Donati family, 58, 79

Donati, Buoso, 2

Donati, Corso, 79, 110

Donati, Forese, 62, 79, 110, 147, 162

Donati, Gemma, 26, 153

Donati, Piccarda, *see* Piccarda Donati

Dunbar, H. F., 149; quoted, 150–51

Earthly Paradise, 68, 143, 144–45, 152; natural beauty of, 17–18, 51

Ebro river, 131

Ecclesiasticus, quoted, 138

Eliot, T. S., cited, 7, 64; quoted, 22

Emilia, Italy, 59

Emperor, The, *see* Frederick II, Holy Roman Emperor

Ensenhamen d'onor (Sordello), 107–108, 109

Envy, sin of, 75, 122

Epicurus, 58

Epistolae (Dante), 144

Este, Obizzo d', 3

Eurydice, 88

Eve, 15, 67, 68, 70

Evil, 75–76; characterization and, 12–15, 16, 120; Church corruption, 97, 139–41; degrees of, 53, 125, 126; feminine, 67–71, 76, 152, 153; salvation and, 10, 81, 120–22, 135;

Tuscan sins, 58–59, 62, 64, 72–73, 152–53, 156. *See also specific sins*

Ezzelino da Romano, 80, 104, 109, 119–20, 122

Faenza, Italy, 59

Falsehood, 2–3, 53, 62, 70; false-counselors, 63, 102; hypocrisy, 54, 55, 71; lust and, 60

Farinata degli Uberti, 14, 19, 70, 79, 89, 122; Dante conversation with, 119, 157, 158, 163; Sordello and, 93, 110

Feltre, Italy: bishop of, 125, 126

Ferrara, Italy, 106, 124, 125

Ferrers Howell, A. G., quoted, 106–107

Flamini, F., 47, 108; quoted, 112

Flattery, 70, 71

Florence, Italy, 145–46; Cacciaguida and, 4, 19, 38, 146, 148, 151–56, 162–163; Charles Martel in, 24; Cunizza's death in, 121; hell and, 58–59, 62, 64; emigration to, 37, 38, 43; Mars and, 139, 163; political life of, 8–9, 26–27, 37, 40–41, 44, 154–55, 163; prophecy against, 113, 116–17, 140

Folquet de Marseille, 4, 80, 102, 114, 123; Arnaut Daniel and, 21, 93, 96, 127; Crusades and, 97–98, 133–34, 138–39, 140; Guiraut de Bornelh and, 99–100, 101; Rahab and, 79, 97, 113, 136–39; rhetoric of, 99, 115, 122, 128–30, 131–37, 139–40

Forese Donati, 62, 79, 110, 147, 162

Foster, Kenelm, quoted, 161

France, 153; Avignonnais papacy of, 8–9, 27; Crusades and, 97

Francesca da Rimini, 3, 12–14, 60, 70, 71; Cunizza and, 19, 82, 84–85, 120, 121, 122; Pia and, 75; Sayers on, 83–84; Ugolino and, 57, 62, 162

Franciscan order, 9

Fraticelli, Pietro, cited, 90

Fraud, sin of, 54–55, 58, 60

Frederick II, Holy Roman Emperor, 107; Constance and, 21, 77, 110; Farinata and, 79; on nobility, 41–42; Pier della Vigna and, 15, 59

Free will doctrine: circles of Heaven and, 137; divine judgment and, 10,

Free will doctrine (*cont'd*)
18; government and, 38; Purgatory and, 16, 17
Fucci, Vanni, 61, 70
Furies, 2, 61

Gabriel, Archangel, 140
Gardner, Edmund, cited, 81–82
Garigliano river, 59
Gawain, 88
Gemma Donati, wife of Dante, 26, 153
Genoa, Italy, 58, 97, 131, 133
Gentile, G., cited, 110; quoted, 103, 107
Georgics (Virgil), 88
Ghibellines, 9, 27, 162; Cunizza da Romano and, 81, 119, 121, 122, 123–127, 139; Treviso and, 125
Gianciotto da Rimini, 14, 62, 84, 120
Giants, 61
Gluttony, sin of, 51–52, 60, 71, 76, 147, 152
God, 81, 97, 135, 166; justice of, 10, 18, 19, 77, 117, 121, 122, 126–27, 135, 141; love and, 20–21, 84
Godfrey of Bouillon, 160, 161
Goito, Italy, 81, 102, 103, 104
Grabher, Carlo, cited, 157
Grandgent, C. H., quoted, 94, 95
Gray, Thomas, 16
Gregory, saint, 127
Greece, 59
Guarnerio, P. E., cited, 108
Guelph-Ghibelline controversy, 9, 119, 162; Cunizza's prophecy and, 81, 121, 122, 123–27, 139; Sordello and, 108, 109; White Guelphs, 27, 153
Guido del Duca, 41
Guinevere and Launcelot legend, 13, 14
Guinizelli, Guido, 13, 66; on Arnaut Daniel, 93, 94, 127
Guiraut de Bornelh, 87, 99–100, 101
Guiscard, Robert, 160, 161

Harpies, 61
Hatzfeld, H., quoted, 75
Heaven, *see Paradiso*
Hebrews, book of, cited, 138
Hebrus river, 88

Hector, 160
Hecuba, 2
Helen of Troy, 12
Hell, *see Inferno*
Henry VII, Holy Roman Emperor, 27, 141
Henry III, king of England, 107
Henry Plantagenet, son of Henry II, king of England, 89, 90, 92
Hercules, 133
Heresy, 52–63, 133–34; Catharist, 9, 97–98; Tuscany and, 58
Hoare, Alfred, 91
Homer, 57, 110
Hypocrisy, sin of, 54, 55, 71

Imagery, 4, 22, 128; battlefield, 90, 91, 92, 129; cross, 145, 149, 150, 159, 163, 164, 166; eagle, 163; fire, 120, 130, 146; landscape, 16–18, 50–55, 164; lion, 150; ruby, 127–28, 164; serpent, 103; severed head, 88–89; urban, 35, 39–40, 50, 52, 55; water of salvation, 136
Imola, Italy, 106
Inconstancy, sin of, 76
Incontinence, sin of, 58
Inferno, 47–64, 90, 128, 129, 130; *Ensenhamen* of Sordello and, 108; Florentine politics and, 37, 119, 151, 154–55, 156; population of, 1–3, 4, 11–15, 16, 21, 48, 49–50, 52–53, 54, 56–64, 70–71, 79, 81, 82, 88, 93, 119–120, 122, 135, 148, 149, 154–55, 156, 157, 159, 160, 163; topography of, 3, 10, 12, 48, 49–56, 64, 70, 110, 115, 119, 144; thematic unity in, 113–114, 144; Virgin Mary and, 21
Iole, 132, 133
Irving, Washington, "The Legend of Sleepy Hollow" of, 88
Isolde, 13, 14

Jacopone da Todi, quoted, 25
James, saint, cited, 138
Jason, 57, 89
Jericho, 138
Jerome, saint, 67
Jerusalem, 131
Jesus Christ, 45, 140, 146, 157; figures of, 137, 138, 149–51; Second Coming, 123

Johannes de Garlandia, 133
John Lackland, king of England, 89, 90
Joshua, 97, 137, 138, 160; book of, cited, 138
Joyce, James, cited, 88
Judaeo-Christian tradition, 3, 56–57, 60. *See also* Catholicism
Judas, 56, 60
Judas Maccabee, 160
Julius Caesar, 4, 132, 160
Juno, 1
Jupiter, 19, 141, 142
Justice: divine, 10, 18, 19, 21, 77, 117, 121, 122, 126–27, 135, 141; hierarchy and, 43–44, 77
Justinian, 130, 152

Körting, Gustav, 91
Kuhns, L. O., quoted, 53

Lana, Jacopo della, cited, 135
Language, 22, 27, 57, 93–96, 100, 112; Adam and, 68; baby talk, 4; of Cacciaguida, 147, 148–49, 151, 152, 159, 163–66; of Folquet de Marseille, 99, 115, 122, 128–30, 131–37, 139–40; Italian choice, 5, 7–8; linguistic study, 29, 114–15; narrative and, 117–18, 144, 159–60; neologisms, 91–92, 99, 115, 123, 129–30; of Plutus, 61; *re giovane* dispute, 89, 90; Sordello use of, 102–103, 106–107; sphere of Venus and, 141–142
Langue d'oc, *see* Provençal
Languedoc, France, 97
Latin, 5, 7, 9, 102; Cacciaguida and, 147, 148–49, 151; Dante works in, 29; Latinisms, 123, 160
Latini, Brunetto, 4, 9, 54, 62, 64, 127, 147, 157; Cacciaguida and, 93, 159, 162, 163
Latium, 59
Launcelot and Guinevere legend, 13, 14, 94
Laura, Petrarch's, 67
Lazzari family, 61
Le dolci rima (Dante), 100
Learchus, son of Athamas, 1
Lethe river, 51, 111, 135

Liguria, Italy, 59, 131
Limbo, 12, 50–51, 53, 54, 55, 59, 70; Aeneas in, 149; children in, 60; garden of princes and, 110, 111; visit of Beatrice, 62
Loderingo degli Andolò, 62
Lollis, Cesare de, cited, 100
Lombardo, Marco, 36, 38–39
Lombardy, Italy, 59, 103, 109
Louis X, king of France, 116
Love, 7, 10, 11, 12, 30, 44; as civic virtue, 35, 39, 40; courtly, 13–14, 28, 65–66, 67–68, 81, 134; Dante's view of, 70–71, 83, 84; divine, 20–21, 45–46, 79; justice and, 141; medieval view of, 13–14, 28, 60, 65–66, 67–68, 81; ruby emblem of, 127–28; as subject of poetry, 87, 97, 98–99, 100–101, 122, 133, 134; as union, 129–30
Lowell, James Russell, 8; quoted, 155
Lucan, 132
Lucca, Italy, sinners of, 57–58, 59
Lucia, saint, 65
Lucifer, *see* Satan
Lust, 12, 15, 16, 51, 52; egotism and, 84, 85, 141; feminine, 60, 71, 76; salvation and, 81, 120–22, 135, 136, 137, 141; violence and, 70–71
Lyric tradition, 9, 21, 26; courtly love and, 13, 66, 67–68; Provençal sources, 87–111

Macbeth, Lady, 71
Maccabee, Judas, 160
Machiavelli, Nicolò, 37
Macra river, 131
Malacoda, 61
Malagoli, L., quoted, 48
Malaspina, Currado, 157
Malebolge, 54–55, 58, 63, 90, 102, 114
Malebranche, 4, 55, 61, 63
Malory, Thomas, *Morte d'Arthur* of, 160
Malta, 124, 125
Mandelshtam, Osip, cited, 172n17; quoted, 164
Manfred, king of Naples and Sicily, 21, 79, 93, 110, 122; defeat of, 27
Mangone, Italy, 81
Manto, 59, 60, 70, 157
Mantua, Italy, 104, 106

Marche of Italy, 59; Trevisana, 119, 124-25
Maremma, 53, 54, 74
Marigo, Aristide, cited, 105, 107
Mars, 139; sphere of, 143-66
Marseilles, France, 97, 131-32, 133
Mary, Virgin, *see* Virgin Mary
Massa Marittima, Italy, 74
Matelda, 65, 71, 111
Mazzeo, J. A., quoted, 149
Mediterranean Sea, 131, 132
Medusa, 61
Menzini, B., cited, 91
Mercury, sphere of, 130, 137
Meyer-Lübke, Wilhelm, 91
Middle Ages, 7, 8, 31; ascetic traditions of, 25-26, 45; cities of, 52; courtesy books of, 108; nine worthies of, 160; verse traditions of, 22, 154; view of government in, 40, 43; view of women in, 13-14, 28, 65-66, 67-68, 71; witches, 60
Miei sirventes vuolh far de·ls res amdos (Bertran de Born), 91
Miniato, saint, 88
Modena, Italy, 106
Mohammed, 88, 92
Momigliano, Attilio, 93, 123; quoted, 73, 116, 152
Monarchia, De (Dante Alighieri), 29-30, 43; didacticism of, 5, 35, 47, 101
Monarchy, 141, 145, 150, 151; Cacciaguida and, 152, 153; Ghibelline prophecy of Cunizza and, 81, 121, 122, 123-27, 139; hereditary, 24-25, 41, 43, 103, 115-16; imperialist, 29-30, 39-40, 107, 109, 124, 125, 163; papal power and, 8-9, 27, 30, 39, 163
Montano, Rocco, quoted, 159
Montefeltro, Bonconte da, 74, 119, 121
Montefeltro, Guido da, 114, 121, 154
Moon, 76, 130, 137
Moors (Saracens), 98, 161
Morte d'Arthur, Le (Malory), 160
Mosca degli Uberti, 3, 88
Murder, 63, 64, 126
Music, 145, 146, 150-51
Myrrha, 60, 70, 71; Gianni Schicchi and, 2, 3, 4, 57

Naples, kingdom of, 24, 116, 139
Narrative, 10-11, 36, 47-48; allegory and, 16-17, 18, 22-23, 30, 48, 64, 102, 110-11, 157; synthesis in, 3, 56-57, 59; verse form and, 117-18, 129, 144, 159-60
Nationalism, *see* Monarchy, imperialist
Nazareth, 140
Nello de' Pannocchieschi, 74, 75
New Testament, 57, 140
Nimrod, 61
"Nine Worthies," 160-61
Nino Visconti, 68-69, 70, 76, 125
Novello, Alesandro, bishop of Feltre, 125, 126
Numerology, 63

Old Testament, 57, 60, 76, 138, 152, 156. *See also specific Books*
Orlando, 160
Orpheus, 88
Ottimo commento della Divina Commedia, 120-21, 135
Ovidio, Francesco d', cited, 140

Padua, Italy, 59, 124, 125, 126
Paganism, 2, 15, 139, 149; Dante's view of, 17, 160
Pandering, sin of, 55, 58, 61
Paolo, 12, 58, 84. *See also* Francesca da Rimini
Papacy, 30, 39; Avignonnais, 8, 9, 27, 141; Crusades and, 97, 98, 134, 138, 139-40, 163
Papini, Giovanni, cited, 8, 155
Paradise, terrestrial, *see* Earthly Paradise
Paradiso, 36, 48, 56; Eliot on, 64; outcasts from, 61; population of, 15, 18-19, 21, 49, 62, 71, 76-82, 84-85, 96-99, 101-102, 108, 113, 115-123, 133-36, 137, 138-39, 143, 145, 156, 160, 164; sphere of Mars, 143-166; sphere of Venus, 112-42, 144; topography of, 10, 16, 19-20, 24, 49, 50, 127, 137, 144-46; unity and, 128, 129-30, 144
Paris, 12
Parodi, E. G., cited, 154
Paul, saint, 36; Aeneas and, 148, 149, 163; on sex, 67

Pazzi family, 58
Pazzi, Carlino de', 62
Per solatz revelhar (Guiraut de Bornelh), 100
Petrarch (Francesco Petrarca), 44, 67, 133, 166; quoted, 25–26
Petrose (Dante Alighieri), 94, 101
Pharsalia (Lucan), 132
Philosophy, 101, 110, 112
Phyllis, 133
Pia de' Tolomei, 71, 73–75, 82, 85, 93
Piave river, 80, 119
Piccarda Donati, 4, 85, 130, 151; Constance and, 77–79, 80, 110; on God's will, 18, 76–77, 81
Pier da Medicina, 57
Pier Pettinaio, 72, 73
Pier della Vigna, 15, 59, 62, 93, 99; violence and, 64, 70
Piero, 54
Pietrobono, L., cited, 130
Pietro di Dante, 116, 120
Pisa, Italy, 59
Pistoia, Italy, 59, 61
Plutus, 61
Poetry, canto divisions and, 113–14, 156; *dolce stil nuovo* of, 18, 93–96, 109; lyric traditions, 9, 13, 21, 26, 66, 67–68, 87–111; rhyme patterns, 5, 21–22, 94, 95, 99, 115, 136, 138, 139. *See also* Language
Polydorus, 2
Polyxena, 2
Pompey, 132
Porena, M., 105
Poscia ch'amor (Dante), 100
Potiphar's wife, 60
Pound, Ezra, quoted, 90, 95
Predestination doctrine, 19, 21, 85
Pride, sin of, 16, 75, 76, 122, 154
Provençal, 9, 21; troubadour traditions, 66–67, 68, 81, 87–111, 128–30, 134, 154, 155
Provençe, France, 104
Provenzal, Dino, 73, 75, 152, 153
Pulci, Luigi, 94
Purgatorio, 20, 48, 57, 64; on aristocracy, 41, 42, 110, 125; Dante's role in, 15–18, 19, 36, 159, 161–62; language in, 4, 148; population of, 15–18, 21, 59, 60, 62, 68–69, 71–76,

79, 81, 93, 101, 102–11, 122, 125, 127, 129, 156; topography of, 10, 11, 16–18, 20, 49, 50, 110, 144; the upper world and, 45, 56, 152, 164

Quasimodo, Salvatore, quoted, 32, 49

Rahab, 141; Folquet de Marseille and, 79, 97, 113, 136–39
Ravenna, Italy, 8, 27
Raymond Berenger IV, 104
Raymond of Foix, 133–34
Remediis, De (Petrarch), 67
Reynouard, 160–61
Rhone (Rodano) river, 52
Rialto, Italy, 79, 80, 118
Rimini, Francesca da, *see* Francesca da Rimini
Rimini, Gianciotto da, 14, 62, 84, 120
Rinaldo (prose romance), 94
Ripheus, 62
Robert, king of Naples, 24, 116
Roland, 160
Romagna, Italy, 41, 57, 59, 154
Romano family, 119. *See also* Cunizza da Romano; Ezzelino da Romano
Rome, Italy: Church of, 97, 140; world monarchy and, 30, 40, 43
Roncaglia, E., 84*n*
Rougemont, Denis de, cited, 14
Rusticucci, Jacopo, 119

Saladin, 104, 106
Samson, 137
San Benedetto, Italy, 56
San Bonifazio, Ricciardo di, 104, 120
Santangelo, S., cited, 90, 100–101, 105
Sapegno, Natalino, cited, 90, 95, 96, 105, 107, 135, 153; quoted, 73, 116, 143
Sapia, 4, 56, 71–73, 85
Saracens (Moors), 98, 161
Sardinia, 58, 59
Satan, 10, 53, 57, 61, 105; Florence and, 139; treason and, 62
Savonarola, Girolamo, 37
Sayers, Dorothy, quoted, 48, 83–84
Scala, Francesco della (Can Grande), 10, 124, 150
Scartazzini, G. A., cited, 83, 121; quoted, 80, 97, 117, 135
Schiaffini, A., cited, 91

Schicchi, Gianni, 2, 3, 4, 57
Science, 30, 110, 115, 136; astronomical, 137, 145–46, 150
Scipio, 148
Semele, 1
Semiramis, 12, 14, 59, 70
Seneca, 145
Shakespeare, William, 11, 71
Sicily, kingdom of, 161
Siena, Italy, 72–73, 74
Sile river, 124, 125
Simony, 53, 55, 71
Sin, *see* Evil; *and see specific sins*
Sinon, 57, 62
Si tuit li dol e·lh plor e·lh marrimen (Bertran de Born), 90
Sloth, sin of, 75, 76
Sodomy, 62, 63
Solomon, 4
Soothsaying, 55, 60, 70, 71
Sophocles, 57
Sordello, 42, 93, 102–11, 129; Cunizza da Romano and, 81, 104, 108–109, 120, 122
Speculum morale (Vincent of Beauvais), 133
Spitzer, Leo, cited, 91
Statius, Publius Papinius, 18, 22, 93
Steiner, Carlo, quoted, 143
Stroński, S., quoted, 98, 99, 134
Styx river, 52
Suicide, sin of, 15
Swabian royal house, 58, 79, 161

Tagliamento river, 123
Tan m'abellis l'amoros pensamen (Folquet de Marseille), 99
Tasso, Torquato, 94
Tertullian, 67
Terza rima form, 5, 21–22
Thaïs, 60, 70
Thebes, 1, 2, 64
Theft, 53, 54, 55, 62; serpent metamorphosis, 63; women and, 71
Thomas Aquinas, saint, 8, 9, 48; on eternity, 61–62; on Thrones of Justice, 127; on women, 67
Thrones, Choir of, 126–27
Toja, Gianluigi, cited, 94
Torraca, F., cited, 105, 108
Tosa, Pino della, 125
Tosinghi family, 154

Trajan, 62, 141
Treason, sin of, 58, 60, 62; clerical, 126, male quality of, 71
Tre donne intorno al cor (Dante), 100
Trent, Italy, 53, 55
Treviso, Italy, 120; *marche* of, 119, 124–25
Tristram and Isolde legend, 12, 13, 14
Triumphiis ecclesiae libri octo, De (Johannes de Garlandia), 133
Troubadours, 60, 81, 87–111, 122, 127, 132, 139; courtly love and, 66–67, 68, 134; sirvente form and, 154
Troubadours of Dante (Chaytor), 90
Tuscany, 8, 131; sinners of, 58–59, 62, 64, 72–73, 152–53, 156. *See also* Florence, Italy

Ubaldini family, 58
Uberti family, 154
Uberti, Farinata degli, *see* Farinata degli Uberti
Ugolino de' Gherardeschi, 57, 60, 62, 162
Uguccione della Faggiuola, 116
Ulysses, 57, 60, 89, 102, 114; Diomed and, 62
Usury, 62

Valli, L., cited, 162
Vandelli, G., cited, 95
Vanni Fucci, 61, 70
Vatican, *see* Papacy, The
Veltro, 141
Venice, Italy, 59
Ventadorn, Bernart de, 98, 133
Venus, 112–42; Folquet de Marseille in, 21, 79, 80, 96–99, 129–30, 137, 139; sphere of, 24, 71, 76, 79–82, 114, 127
Verona, Italy, 27, 106, 107, 120, 165
Vicenza, Italy, 124, 125, 126
Vidal, Peire, 133
Villani, Giovanni, quoted, 27–28, 120
Vincent of Beauvais, 133
Violence, sin of, 53–54, 63–64, 119–20, 147; Tuscany and, 58; women and, 60, 70–71
Virgil, 9, 93, 154, 162; Beatrice and, 62, 145, 158, 161; narrative use of, 10, 11, 12, 15, 17, 18, 22, 30, 36, 49,

Virgil (*cont'd*)
55, 56, 57, 110, 157; on Orpheus, 88; Sordello and, 103, 105, 110; Ulysses and, 114; Virgin Mary and, 21; worldly fame and, 123
Virgin Mary, 4, 65, 67; intercessions of, 21
Viscardi, L., cited, 94, 109
Visdomini family, 154
Vitaliano del Dente, 62
Vita nuova, La (Dante Alighieri), 10, 26, 29, 34; Beatrice and, 28, 30, 47; hermeticism of, 32–33; Provençal poetry and, 90, 93
Viterbo, Italy, 125
Vossler, Karl, 90; quoted, 141, 163
Vulgari eloquentia, De (Dante Alighieri), 5, 29, 89, 95, 114; didacti-

cism of, 35, 47; on speech, 68; on themes of poetry, 87, 90; on the troubadours, 94, 98, 99, 100, 101, 106, 134

Whites, *see* Guelph-Ghibelline controversy
William of Orange, 160
William of Poitou, 67, 98, 133; quoted, 66
Williams, Charles, 48
Wrath, sin of, 16, 52, 75, 76

Youth, virtues of, 34–35

Zingarelli, Nicola Antonio, cited, 107, 133, 138